Life and Death in Nanking

PEGGY KORDICK

Baltimore, Maryland

Life and Death in Nanking

Library of Congress
Cataloging-in-Publication Data
ISBN 1-56167-824-4

Library of Congress Card Catalog Number:
2003094730

Published by

8019 Belair Road, Suite 10
Baltimore, Maryland 21236

Manufactured in the United States of America

FOREWORD

ABOUT PEGGY

She was one of those idealistic teenagers of the thirties and forties, full of naive ideas on how to solve the world's problems. Her background? Small town, minister's daughter, Iowa, WASP. But from an education-oriented family.

She left after two years of college because her family couldn't handle even minimal expenses for two children seeking higher knowledge at once. That fall, (1941) she headed for Washington, D.C.

The world was in a mess: WWII was whirling closer for Americans, but she had a BALL! Everything was new and exciting. Everything had to be shared with the benighted folk back home.

She started as a babysitter/housekeeper for a couple in government jobs. Her bug-eyed curiosity had her standing beside (Secretary of State) Cordell Hull's car listening to the report of the bombing of Pearl Harbor, then staring at Japanese diplomats scrambling down the State Department's steps to their cars and a hasty get-away.

Washington grew more frenzied as the nation put on battle-dress. She got a job at the FBI as a lowly file clerk, but was convinced she was helping the war effort.

One night at eleven, she was summoned before the awesome presence of J. Edgar Hoover to account for her missing ID badge. It had slipped off her lap into the Tidal Basin while she had been on a date with a land-locked Navy Ensign. Laughingly, she remarked that surely no spy would find it there. Hoover crushed her with the comment: "Young lady, you obviously do not take your responsibility seriously."

How could he DARE say that?

She dated a lot. Sang for the FBI Recreational Association. Sang for the Police Academy. Sang for the USO. Also she sang in a church choir. In the fall of 1942, she married the assistant minister of that church and resigned from the "Bureau."

The following November (1943), a son was born to the couple, now in residence in Berkeley, California as missionaries in training for service in China. In addition to household duties, she studied Chinese and completed her college degree at UCB.

The war ended. In January of 1946, Ben, her husband, sailed for China. In July, a daughter was born. On December ninth, she and Tom, two and a half, and Judy, five months, sailed toward an unknown adventure in China.

The letters which follow, saved methodically by her parents, tell what happened.

TABLE OF CONTENTS

LIFE AND DEATH IN NANKING

Aboard the GENERAL GORDON
Saturday, Dec. 21, 1946

If you could see the difficulties under which I'm writing, you'd know how desperate I am to get this letter written. I'm seated sideways on a stack of suitcases in our "Stateroom," leaning over a pile of clothes to reach the table. Tom is running in and out and Judy is squalling in the buggy behind me. That's the picture.

The *General Gordon* is rolling deeply, but things are supposed to calm down by tonight as we pass close to the islands of Japan. We average nearly 500 miles each day, but the typhoon which hit us last Tuesday slowed us and made the trip most unpleasant. It has been scary. More about that later, first some history.

After we had stood outside watching the tug, which brought five late passengers, and after we passed under Golden Gate Bridge, we went inside. My arms ached from holding Judy so long. Dinner was served at 5:30, but by the time we were admitted, it was 6:30 and my tummy was rejecting the idea of food. I soon lost the little I swallowed. By the next evening we were well out of the coastal swells, and food tasted OK.

The first week was uneventful, really fun at times, although a twenty-four-hour vigil over two children is exhausting. There is no one to help. If we ever reach Shanghai, I'm going to bed for a month!

This ship is filthy, simply because it is overcrowded. Last night was the first time I've been able to find a seat in the lounge. Some privilege! So many drab, tired people, so much smoke, dirt, papers on the floor, etc. that I could scarcely stand it. In our cabin there are nineteen of us, counting Tom, Judy, and two other children. We have two Chinese, five Filipinos, one English woman and eleven Americans. Normally, this size cabin would hold two people. When several are seasick at once it is awful. There is no place elsewhere fit for children, so I keep Judy in here most of the time.

Everyone treats Tom like someone out of a comic book. Our table in the dining room is next to that of four nuns. The first night, after staring solemnly at their wide, white starched collars, he asked one of them, "Don't you ever get your bib dirty?"

On Sunday there was a Mass for the eighty or so Roman Catholic priests and nuns early in the morning. Tom had disappeared from our cabin, but I thought little of it until one of the nuns said to me at breakfast: "Do you know where your little boy was this morning?" When I turned to him he said: "Dose men in de pretty dresses were habing a happy birfday, so I blew out de candles." Poor little Protestant! He had no idea of the uproar he had caused. When I sang a solo at our services later I kept one eye on him to keep him in line.

About the typhoon! It struck just as Tom and I were on our way to breakfast Tuesday morning. (We skipped from Sunday to Tuesday). The ship began to lurch and pitch and roll and jump and shake until I thought it would fall apart. It rolled so deeply from side to side that the wall was often where you'd expect the floor to be. The dishes were all broken in the dining room and scores of passengers and sixteen crew members were seriously injured. One elderly Chinese man died and one woman had several ribs broken. A small boy had the back of his head cut open.

The passengers were asked to stay either in bed or in one place so the crew could move more easily about. No meals were served, but the stewards came around with sweet rolls and oranges for breakfast and sandwiches, coffee, and hard boiled eggs later. Bathroom doors were fastened open because they are made of heavy steel and might crash against us. One time, when I was going down the hall, a steward was heading towards me carrying a large tray of sweet rolls. As he passed the women's room, the ship suddenly lurched, flinging him through the open door and tossing his tray and the rolls into lavatories and booths.

The storm was a new experience for me. One hundred mile an hour winds making huge waves. I wasn't too frightened except when we would seem to fly through the air and then hit with a jarring SMACK which made the whole ship shudder.

Towards evening we were told that we had passed the worst part, and by morning things were quite peaceful. That afternoon, however, we got back into it and it has been terribly rough ever since. This afternoon, though, we started ripping along over water as calm as on a lake. We are only about two hundred miles off the coast of Japan, and are in the "shore calms," whatever they are.

Since we have lost so much time in these days of storms, our arrival in Shanghai will not be until December 24th—Christmas Eve! Several of our passengers have made this trip often in the past, and all agree this has been the roughest Pacific crossing they have ever seen. Aren't we the lucky ones?

PEGGY KORDICK

Nanking, China
Sunday, January 1947

When we arrived in Shanghai harbor at two p.m. on December 21, I was exhausted. The customs men had boarded the ship out at the mouth of the Whangpoo River at nine that morning. We were told that when the greenish-blue ocean water began to look more like coffee with cream in it that would be the mouth of the Whangpoo. Sure enough, though there was no other sign that we had arrived, a launch showed up with officials in it. It pulled alongside, the men boarded, and from then on was one big rat race.

I stood in one line for passport checking, another for health check, and a third for hand baggage examination. It sounds simple enough, but was far from it, when you reckon in Judy and Tom. I held her and watched him. No one could spare time to help.

We moved slowly on the Whangpoo towards Shanghai. After we docked at the wharf I peered over the railing at the immense crowd down below. As far as I could tell no one had come to meet us. My baggage had been stacked on the deck on the side opposite the wharf, so I had to keep running back and forth, looking for Ben and keeping an eye on baggage.

At last an old friend showed up to help us, but not before I had shelled out nine U.S. dollars to a coolie; I had decided that was the only way we could get off! It was three times too much, but I was desperate.

Finally we got down the gangplank. Our friend Chuck held one bag and Tom. I carried Judy. Roy Creighton from the Presbyterian mission met us down below, and went looking for a taxi while we stood by a big iron gate to wait. The smells and the noise were fierce! Opposite us were about fifty Chinese men pushing and shoving for a look at the children.

The taxi took us all the way to South Gate to a mission residence on the campus of Mary Farnum Girls' School. By the time we got there it was dark. We unloaded ourselves and our bags, then were escorted up a long flight of stairs to the second floor of that huge, old mission house. Ben greeted us from bed with a sepulchral voice and a deep, hoarse cough. There were no lights, and it was cold, but we were glad to be there anyway. Ben had been forced to bed after dragging around with near-pneumonia for over a week.

The next day was Christmas, so we (Tom and I) sat with the missionary family while they opened their presents. We had none, of course, but Tom was happy when they handed him a package. I was horrified, then angry, to realize that it contained a lump of coal. They all laughed. Welcome to China. Or welcome to missionary humor. Ugh!

At nine the next morning I left for the wharf again to get my trunks through Customs. It took two miserable, icy, rainy, exhausting days, but I got them through without paying any duty by giving the inspector a copy of "Harmony in Marriage," which he seemed to think was fascinating, and inviting him to Nanking to dinner some time. The intense, wet cold at the wharf left me with painful chilblains on fingers and toes, so I hobble like an amah with bound feet, and cannot bear any pressure on fingers.

Saturday afternoon Tom had a fever of 102° but nevertheless we left at six a.m. Sunday to catch the seven a.m. Nanking express train. They were REALLY RUDE about shoving us out so they could get the room ready for their friends due to arrive on the Marine Lynx. I'll try never to make anyone feel like they did me.

When we got on the train we were supposed to have had four seats but two were taken by three Chinese. Ben threw a fit, (the accepted method of getting results here) and, after both he and the three Chinese had made lengthy speeches to the gaping crowd, the Chinese picked up their stuff and moved happily to the seats they were supposed to have had all the time! Crazy business.

The train seemed crawling with germs to me, but Ben assured me it was the cleanest in China. The seats were Pullman style, facing one another, and two of them were occupied by elderly Chinese men. One of them coughed in our faces and spat on the floor or on my feet if I didn't move quickly when he leaned forward.

Judy was a constant source of wonder to all. When I pulled out a bottle to feed her, the aisles were blocked ten feet in both directions. Ben said the people were disappointed that I didn't nurse her, but it would have stopped the train if I had. We opened tins of Army K rations and ate a little bit, but it didn't taste very good. I held Judy, and Tom stretched out and slept a lot.

At the start of the trip we "rented" covered glasses which were soon filled with boiling water and tea grounds which looked more like shredded cabbage. At ten-minute intervals thereafter a man came through and filled these glasses with boiling water from a long-spouted brass kettle.

I made one trip to the public toilet used by both men and women and that was plenty! Shanghai had been so cold that I had to wear two pair of long cotton hose, plus wool anklets, my flannel pajamas, wool slacks, two wool sweaters, a jacket and my red coat, a wool scarf and mittens. Enough said. My feet stayed cold in spite of all that!

We were an hour late in arriving at Nanking, but Dr. Mills and Commander Hackler; a Naval Attache, met us with a U.S. Embassy station wagon. Nanking, even at first glance, was different from Shanghai. Everything looked grimy and gray, dust swirling everywhere. I saw no beggars in Shanghai, but met them at once here. They dress in tatters which flap in the wind, have obviously diseased bodies, and sit by the roadside or run after us as we pass by.

When we stopped at the gate in front of "our" house a crowd of Chinese people had already gathered. With priceless smiles they opened the gate and then lit strings of firecrackers which all had to explode before we could enter. Tom was frightened, and I didn't know quite which way to turn, but soon we entered the gate into our "compound" to find Martha Jones and Sally Wylie there to greet us.

Although the whole house had been painted and somewhat repaired, my first impression was of its complete bareness. Huge gaping curtainless windows, floors scrubbed, but innocent of any varnish or wax, a weird assortment of broken chairs, etc. Our beds are the iron, hospital type, except for Judy's, and hers is an ancient one found in another mission house. When my freight arrives we'll have better ones. There is no furniture here which belongs to us. One by one the pieces we have will be claimed when their owners return in the coming months.

Our house was built by Samuel Mills and lived in (until the Japanese took it over) by Dr. Plumer Mills and family. During the war it was occupied by a general in the Japanese Air Force who did a lot of things (such as digging air raid shelters in the front yard, putting up a four car garage on one corner of the lot, turning flower beds into graveled driveways, etc.) to make it more useful to him. What he did not do, and consequently what we now must do, was anything to keep the place in repair. Walls and ceilings were allowed to crumble away, the plaster dust, unswept, ground into floors, along with indescribable amounts of dirt. Rats apparently marched unchallenged throughout the house, judging by the number of doors, cupboards, etc. with ragged, gnawed sills, and by the squeaking and thumping that goes on each night in the walls.

All of Dr. Mills' furniture, curtains, dishes, and books were "removed" by the Japanese, so when my freight finally arrives all the cloth, dishes, pans, etc. will be put to good use.

Monday both children ran high temperatures, and Tuesday I did, but we all recovered quickly enough. Mine was accompanied by a severely sore throat, which just today left me. It moved over to make room for the stomach upset I have now! Life is not dull. It is cold, and I mean cold. There is no heat, you see, there is a small coal heater which connects with a drum of water in Judy's tiny room, but that is all the heat possible until the blessed day my stuff arrives.

We have three servants: a cook, an amah, and a coolie. We get along fine, but I've not yet taken over the running of the household. By this time next week I hope to be in charge, but have insisted on this time to catch my breath, evolve a routine, and learn. The cook is disappointed, because he wants someone to direct him, but he'll wait. He plans the meals now. Food is good and seemingly plentiful, yet we are hungry all the time, because of the lack of essential vitamins, milk, and fresh vegetables.

Ever since we arrived the house has bristled with carpenters. We found a strange coolie sleeping in the servants' quarters, so put him to work finishing floors all over the house. Tom calls this fellow "You Big Debbel" because we had let that name fly when we discovered the man had been stealing cans of peanuts from our precious supply room.

Tom's attitude toward Chinese people in general is very curious. He bosses them, hits them, and any number of worse things if he isn't stopped. I think it is because he is unable to talk to or understand them. He spends a lot of time watching the stream of people who pass by our front gate. It is fascinating. New Year's there were several lantern parades which were very lovely. So far I have been outside our own gate but twice. Tom and I rode in a rickshaw one night after dark.

Dr. Mills has received us very kindly, though it must be hard for him to give over his home to others. He plans to return to America in May or June. He has been through so much here that he hates to think of leaving. Listening to him reminisce is like reading a book. He has been telling us about the horrors Nanking went through in 1927 and 1937. He is a close friend of Dr. Leighton Stuart, our American Ambassador, and visits him almost daily. Before I arrived this house was the secret meeting place for talks between Dr. Stuart, Mao, George Marshall and others who were trying to get the two main power factions in China together.

So far I've met few Chinese, since my time is spent in unpacking and getting organized for action. Chang Sao Tze, the amah, and I understand one another fairly well. She is around sixty-four, has bound feet, and speaks a very difficult dialect to understand. She thumps painfully over our bare floors, swishing a rag mop which she rinses in a cistern located under the kitchen sink. The idea is not so much to clean the floors as to simply keep the dust down.

Well, there's much more to be said, but I guess I cannot hope to share every new experience with you. It is all very overwhelming right now, and seems to take a lot of adjustment. However, don't think I'm not enjoying every minute of it.

I knew it would be tough and I knew it would be thrilling, and I was right both times!

LIFE AND DEATH IN NANKING

Nanking, China
January 14, 1947

My baggage has finally all arrived, and in 100% condition. You remember that big old trunk someone gave me in Berkeley? That happened to be one of those inspected by Chinese Customs. Afterwards they just roped it shut. When it was delivered here, the top was gaping open, and oranges, film, etc. were clearly visible. But nothing had been touched, a miracle when you realize how fast things are stolen around here.

The other night a friend from the Embassy drove us to the Lewis Smythe's for dinner. Sometime during the two hours we were inside, the Embassy Jeep was swiped from the front gate, even though it had an ignition lock on it!

Things have become terribly important. We save everything; string, bits of paper, envelopes, everything. What we do finally discard, the servants carefully gather. Everything I brought is useful in one way or another. There is nothing here. NOTHING, at least in our echelon. Every scrap of cloth and thread, every pin and safety pin must be treasured.

Life is beginning to have some semblance of order once more. Our property is surrounded by an eight-foot gray brick wall, so the children are protected from the traffic and curiosity of the people on the street outside. Our front yard is about a quarter-acre. Then we have a large garden plot flanked by small bamboo trees on the south side of the house, and a small stretch of garden space between the back of the house and the front (street) wall. The house faces our own yard rather than the street. Over the wall, in the direction the house faces, is a Chinese grammar school of the same gray brick as our house. We can hear the children chanting their rote lessons all day long.

Sunday afternoon Dr. Mills stayed with the children while we went to the Twinem Chapel Church service on the campus of Nanking University. There are Chinese language services in the morning, English in the afternoon.

It has been pouring rain ever since I arrived, and Sunday was no exception. We walked over in the rain. And in mud, am I ever glad for those boots I brought! I couldn't navigate in anything else. Mud comes up over one's ankle in places, and the rest of the time splashes that high from passing traffic and one's own footsteps. We rode the two miles home in the big "semi" truck which is the missionaries' only means of transportation. Everyone piles into the back of the thing, and off we go, rain or shine. It's easy enough for us young things, but a little rough on older women particularly, for they have to be hoisted up and in. They don't seem to mind, however.

Are you wondering about our food? It is good, usually, very good. We even had venison twice last week. It is quite common, comes from Formosa. Cabbage, celery, carrots; rice and potatoes are our usual cooked vegetables. We also have lotus root, bamboo shoots, lotus souffle, water chestnut pancakes, and other tasty Chinese vegetables as well. Meats vary. We have eaten chicken (UNRRA tinned), beef roasts, pork of various cuts, and fish. Cook always serves fish whole on a platter: head, tail and all.

Everything seems to taste the same. This I hope to remedy with a greater variety of seasons for Cook to use. There is very little I can teach him about cooking, but the thing is to keep him from knowing that! He serves us from our Montgomery Ward dishes with as great a flourish as though it were crystal ware in a palace. When I look at the patched seat of his pants, I have a pang for him. He is so dignified it seems incongruous.

Before I came, and before the heating stove was hitched up, Ben was going around shivering. Cook came in one day and, with profuse apologies, offered his own coat. He said a foreign friend had given it to him, but he didn't really need it. That is the kind of person he is. He has pulled me out of a jam several times when I was the only one here and a crisis came up because someone who didn't speak English arrived at the door.

There is only one major problem. All his relatives live with him in our servants' quarters, and that causes a definite health hazard. When I take over the management of the household I'll have to get the extras to leave.

The little four-car brick garage that the Japanese kindly built here has been transformed into a lovely place to use as an office and recreation room for students. One week of the constant stream of callers at our door has convinced me of the wisdom of having such a place. Many of these people come in from filthy places, track all sorts of mud and stuff into the living room, then sit there for hours. Unless you have some other place for business callers, you are stuck with them underfoot all the time, and nothing else gets done.

This way, people who come to see Ben will be sent immediately to the office where, to wile away their time, there will be books and magazines in English and Chinese to read. We're also stocking it with games. Callers who come at mealtime can wait there instead of sitting in full view of our table while we eat. They always come at mealtime, since that is the only time they can be sure of finding Dr. Mills and Ben here. No one, of course, wants to see me!

The other morning three middle school students came to the door. Finding it open and no one about, they came right on in. I was using the toilet at the top of the stairs. That door, though closed, was unlocked. The next thing I knew I was staring with severe shock at three startled faces peering at me through the now-open door! I recovered myself enough to order them downstairs. When I got down there myself a few moments later, I found them trying to plug in my little radio without its transformer. They meant no harm, but our student center should prevent such incidents.

We are somewhat more used to the cold now, and have acquired another small stove for the upstairs. When my little kerosene ones come, we'll be hot! Lights are turned off in our section of the city about one night out of four. On those nights we use candles and kerosene lanterns. If the electric service stays this chancy, the appliances I shipped out won't be of much use. Our section of the city is not as vital as some others, so ours is not a priority.

We had anti-foreign demonstrations around New Year's. The students are so wretched physically that they are a tinderbox easily ignited. They are especially ripe for Communist agitation. Some feel that students demonstrate against America, simply because they are frustrated in their desire to demonstrate against their own government. Because the Kucmintang supports the U.S. (and vice versa) that means they can strike against the U.S. as an alternative. In any case, the parades and strikes did not last long this time. Most people are very friendly.

Tomorrow is China New Year, a Grand Slam holiday here, so all the servants get the day off. I'll have my first go at fighting with that funny old stove. Also, we have to dig down and scrape up some cash bonuses for them. Oh, Joy! Money is not something we have a lot of.

Both children are healthy and adjusting better to the events of their days in Nanking. Judy has an incredible appetite. The other day I was giving her some pineapple juice (UNPRA canned) and the Cook informed me that if she were a Chinese baby that that stuff would make her deathly sick. Everything I do for the children is watched and commented upon. They seem to think I'm more than half crazy.

LIFE AND DEATH IN NANKING

Nanking, China
Wednesday, January 29, 1947

Guess who was my star dinner guest last evening? Ambassador Leighton Stuart! And his friend and aide, Philip Fu. We also had Dr. and Mrs. Horton Daniels and a lovely Chinese lady, Ms. Mary Chen, the sister-in-law of the principal of Ming Teh Girls Middle School across the street from us. You can imagine how the dust flew around here while I got things ready. Dr. Stuart is a great man, quiet, reserved, a complete gentleman, dignified and tired. I liked him at once. Philip Fu is from north China, tall and sophisticated, though very courteous.

Mary Chen had brought a few branches of 'lao mei hua' (flowering winter plum) a yellow, fragrant, waxy blossom, a few days ago, so I stuck two of them, Japanese style, in a flat glass bowl. My Montgomery Ward dishes combined beautifully with my silver and other accessories to make as pretty a table as you'd see anywhere. (Well, almost anywhere.)

The menu was tomato juice, dried pea soup, lamb, potatoes, canned asparagus, carrots, apple pie, and coffee. Cook outdid himself on the pies, and made the prettiest I've ever seen. We use dried apple nuggets from UNRRA supplies, and they cook up beautifully. Cook rolls tiny strips of crust and crisscrosses them and then makes a pie crust rose and leaves on top. It's much too pretty to eat, really. He is a magician.

As you probably guessed, our freight finally arrived on Saturday the twenty-fifth. The expressions when things were unpacked were a panic. The electric stove was unveiled between the house and the servants' quarters. When Cook's wife saw it, she came dancing out squealing about the beautiful "do the washing machine." Cook, who had been told what it was, turned scornfully and said, "Quiet, old woman, this is the beautiful new STOVE." And so she squealed more.

The children's toys fascinate them. When the amah first saw the tiny, rubber doll hot water bottle, she bent double laughing. Chinese use them, too. Last evening I tried for fifteen minutes to explain the use of the Cory Coffee maker to Cook, as I wanted it used for dinner. He looked skeptical, and I feared the worst when pie was served and for a few minutes no coffee.

He soon appeared, however, and all was well. This morning, eyes shining, he brought the Cory to me and said, "T'ai T'ai, last night I wondered if you were crazy when you said the water would first go up top, then down bottom, but it did. Wonderful machine." He speaks no English, so explaining such things is pretty rough.

We have begun to distribute the clothes from the barrels I brought out. Some went to the eighth child of a Chinese pastor. He and his wife had us over for lunch Monday, and therein hangs another tale.

This was my debut into real Chinese living. This family lives within the compound at Hubugai (across the city), as he is pastor there. Their house, mission-built, is Western-style, but their guests and customs were not. There were sixteen guests in all: elders, deacons and church folk. When we arrived, we were seated around the edge of a large room and served tea and small candies. Not much was said. Women are silent in the presence of men in such a gathering.

As each guest arrived there ensued an argument over the "least worthy" seats. It is a kind of game where guests are expected to look for the worst seats while the host tries to force them into the best ones. (They all looked the same to me.) Anyway, after a while, we filed into another room and seated ourselves around two round tables. Another fight over "least worthy" seats.

Then Chinese dishes were brought in, one or two at a time, the host generously heaping the guests' plates, using his own chopsticks. Ten or eleven dishes were served in all. The climax was a steaming samovar containing a meat omelet floating over soup and noodles. Everyone dived into this up at least to the wrist. For a while there was grave doubt as to whether some might drown or at least be strangled by a neighbor's noodles!

Ben kept up a conversation, but I sat, dumb as could be, taking it all in. I understand much of what is said, but don't say much except to servants as yet.

At the end a servant brought in steaming towels for each guest, (the necessity for them was obvious!) and we were free to leave. We were concerned about this pastor's spending so much to entertain us, but we needn't have been. On our way out, he presented us with the bill!

From your latest letter it seems that you are getting misinformation from somewhere. Dad's remark that: "prices are improving and I hope will continue" left us gasping. Is that what American papers are reporting? If so, that's terrible because it simply is not so.

China's finances are in the most precarious of positions. Any moment may see an economic collapse here, and with it, who knows? Perhaps the government's collapse as well. Cost of living was up twenty-five per cent in February over January's level. We bargain for material one week, and by the next week the cost has doubled, in some cases tripled. Bookkeeping is impossible. The causes and reasons for continuance of the situation are too numerous and complicated for even those here in China to generalize about.

My impressions of China now? I'm still in a watching and listening stage, but before long I'll have to do more than that. I have agreed to give one-hour voice lessons to eight senior music students at Ginling College this semester. Ginling, a first-class girls' school in Nanking, is recognized as a sister school to Smith College in Massachusetts.

My life is occupied with routine tasks: running this household and caring for the children. So far, I've entrusted the amah with very little of the children's care. The amah's days are filled by doing washing and housecleaning, and she is not young. We will have to get a younger amah soon, though I do not plan to "turn the children over" to anyone, ever.

Nanking is a terribly dirty place. The heavy traffic on Moh Tsou Lu (our street) raises a disagreeable cloud of dust on days when the rain and slop-buckets have not reduced the road to puddles of yellow goo. There is a never-ending stream of animal and human traffic on all streets, but particularly on ours. Farmers lead horses or donkeys on the sidewalks, or drive pigs, geese, etc. up and down the roadway.

As for the human traffic, that moves in various ways. There are pedestrians, of course, by the thousands. Then there are people riding in buses, horse-carts, rickshas, pedicabs. Now and then we hear the rhythmic chanting of teams of men bending nearly parallel to the ground, straining to haul loads of wooden poles, racks of hay, or heavy pipes on flat, wooden two-wheeled carts.

A great many men sort of trot and shuffle under the loads they carry in large baskets slung by ropes from bamboo poles balanced across their shoulders. Some of these even carry two charcoal stoves instead of the baskets. Inside these hot stoves are usually steamed sweet potatoes or sesame and onion flavored buns.

Nanking, China
March 1, 1947

This past week we have used the electric stove. Oh, joy! The cook is finally converted. The first night I chanced into the kitchen at six and found nothing doing. Cook was furiously pacing the floor, his wife washing dishes and trying to soothe him.

"What is the matter?" My brilliant question.

"Stove is no blankety-blank good," replies Lu Shih Fu.

"But the electrician said it was working fine."

"Ha!" snarls Cook, pointing to the well-insulated coils, Hot Points pride and joy. "Pu hung!" (They don't get red.)

Soooo, I launched into a sermon on the marvels of modern insulating methods, and advised him to wait a bit after he turned it on and he'd find it hot enough. So he did. But dinner was served at eight-thirty with many reproachful glares at me from not only Cook, but Ben, Dr. Mills, and Ellen Drummond (last week's house guest).

Slowly, Cook is learning to like it though, and he takes great pride in bustling around it when strangers are in the kitchen. Right now the electrician is back trying to get it into better shape than he left it in last week. The electrician is wonderful. He is a teacher (Chinese) and graduate of an electrical school in Chicago.

This week also saw the initiation of the electric sewing machine. I made the downstairs drapes with it, and it was a joy. Mrs. Mills had used a treadle machine, so the amah was awed by this new-fangled gadget. She can't wait to use the washing machine. We haven't figured out how to install that.

We really have a "community problem." Our servants have taken in one person after another until their quarters bulge at the seams. This is funny and sad at once, but cannot be allowed because of the health hazard it creates for us and for them.

They were told to "clean house" before I came, and Dr. Mills' Chinese secretary has served notice on them again since, but more and more strangers have moved in. Last night we called Cook, his wife, and the amah into the living room after dinner for a powwow. Since I am official house-boss now I made a long speech, giving them until next Wednesday to get rid of all outsiders. Then we paid them. We'll see how it works.

My teaching at Ginling College starts next Tuesday. I'm being asked to sing all over the city now, and it is not because my singing is so extra wonderful. There isn't any competition! Those on the staff of the music department at Ginling are either trained only in theory or in instrumental music. So, except for two graduate students who are going to help me, I will be the voice instructor for this semester with the main job of getting these girls ready for their senior recitals.

LIFE AND DEATH IN NANKING

Nanking, China
March 3, 1947

Are you upset by the recent newspaper reports of Communist raids? The situation here is dangerous, but not immediately so. We hope! My main cause for jitters is the children, of course, but after so many here have described the number of times they have been forced to leave the country, returning each time, I am ashamed of myself.

We keep up with what is going on through various sources. We take the Shanghai Evening Post and Mercury newspaper, (English and staffed by Americans and Chinese who know English) and a daily bulletin from the United States Information Service (a branch of the Embassy) which covers political and economic news only, but very thoroughly. Our paper has AP and UP service, including news photos. Last week, for instance, there was a picture of the wreckage of the San Joaquin Daylight train. Most of our news is just a day old, same as yours, and we can hear news broadcasts from the US Army station once an hour, with one broadcast direct from Los Angeles at nine each night. We aren't so far away, really. The Army station also plays Western music all day and picks up Charlie McCarthy, Fibber McGee, the NBC Symphony, etc. and resends them to us. Tom can't stand Chinese music on the radio. He either laughs or yells to cover the sound, or demands that we "turn off that terrible racket."

There are a lot of funny things to be seen and heard. Phonographs on the street blare out a bedraggled version of Auld Lang Syne. On our way to the University we pass a small building with a large sign across its front: FASHION LADIES BEAUTY SALOON.

If we confuse toilets and automobiles with civilization, it would be easy to think China uncivilized. Men, women, and children all use public streets and lots as toilets, so walking is treacherous. Men standing beside walls are not to be stared at. They use all walls as urinals. Women squat in vacant lots or in alleyways. Young children wear trousers with split bottoms. Now that spring is here, it is a common sight to see a circle of little boys, bottoms up, playing marbles in the street. Amah thinks our addiction to diapers exceedingly disgusting!

PEGGY KORDICK

Nanking, China
March 11, 1947

Saturday we had a fascinating experience. We were "welcomed" (to China? to the neighborhood?) at a program put on by the cute children at a poor school down the street from our house. Their songs, stories and dances were all done very well. One tiny girl did a graceful dance to accompany her singing of a Chinese folk song. Her face was sweet, but I could not keep my eyes off the poor little hands: dark purple and lined and seamed like those of an old, old woman. Raw, rubbed places on them from whatever hard manual work she had been forced by her family's poverty to do. A little boy told a story in Chinese, swaggering up to the front, speaking fast and loud and making funny faces all the way back to his seat.

This school is operated by Han Chung Church, next door to us. It was started and is partially funded by our Mission. Our cook's son and the amah's nephew go there. The children are dressed fairly comfortably, but what else they get from the school is doubtful. One thing which is distasteful to us is that the teachers require the children to bow whenever they meet us at school or elsewhere, so the poor little kids spot us a block away and bend double. I hate it. It is more fawning than polite. Anyway, Americans don't like being bowed to especially by tiny children!

This week I've had to tussle with a growing dislike for China. In the first place, China is too overwhelming to merely "like." There are things about it which attract, and many other things which ABSOLUTELY REVOLT ME, and I had never considered myself squeamish or soft. Life is hard here. We live too close to tragedy, sin, suffering, death to honestly be able to disregard the gnawing questions as to the meaning of life itself which, under less chancy circumstances, may be shoved into a back pocket and ignored. There are arrogance, irresponsibility, cruelty, poverty, disease, all around us. I often feel too young and naive to cope. How do we meet such needs without losing our own sanity? God knows. And that is what we have to go on.

Our biggest problem is selecting few enough projects to do adequately. There are huge universities and a number of smaller colleges, not to mention dozens of "middle schools" in the city. Our mission has four fairly large churches, two schools (primary and high school) all crying out for help in this transition period. Our Board has initiated the difficult policy of turning over as much responsibility (financial and administrative) as possible to the Chinese, feeling that our work as leaders is past, and our place now must be more as friends and not-too-vocal advisors.

On the face of it, the job seems to have been simplified. Actually however, it is only more subtle, hence, infinitely more difficult. It would be much easier to rush in and transform young people's organizations in these four churches to a condition more to our standards, using our American methods, but we are expected, rather, to help from within the groups themselves. "Make haste slowly."

Student workers out here (as in America) have used two techniques. One alternative is to form youth fellowships, discussion groups, etc., working from and on the various university campuses. The other is to start a young people's group within the church and make our activities church-centered and church-directed. It is nearly impossible to do both, so a choice is imperative.

Presbyterians used to have a staff of sixty here. At present we are the only ones doing "freelance" work. The rest are all attached to specific institutions. This week the National Christian Council has been here deciding questions involving the disposition of Restoration Fund money.

Here is what is disheartening. The Kiangan Mission gets $210,000 U.S. A lot of money. Yes, Nanking is only one city in that mission and here Presbyterians alone have four churches and numerous other properties. Necessary repairs on ONE church* have been estimated at $130,000 U.S. All we can do is put one foot in front of the other with our hand in God's, because we cannot see very far ahead. But then no one ever has in China.

*Because of war damage.

Nanking, China
March 24, 1947

The afternoon is warm, and Judy and I are sitting beside the house in the sun. She is in her stroller, and I in a folding chair. I'm relaxing after a hard morning at Ginling. At the time my last letter was mailed off to you I was ill, cause unknown, cure the same. I finally managed to wear the thing out, and am rushing about again. Tom, too, has an up and down time of it. Adjustment is not easy.

The Coolie is painting our bamboo fence and gate with green paint scrounged from the U.S. Army, our place looking much better. Trees are at that thrilling leafings out stage. Fruit trees are in bloom around the city, softening the harshness of gray walls and yellow mud.

Sunday afternoon we pedaled outside the city gates. We crossed rice paddies, went through small country villages, through cemeteries, past a lake, over cobbled streets, and back to our door, all in the space of two hours. We rode slowly, too.

We foreigners are so funny to the Chinese. I wore my yellow slacks, and this caused unrestrained comment from the farmers.

"Ai Ya! See the yellow-haired foreign woman in yellow breeches. Ai Ya! Look at the foreign children. Blue eyes. Oh, look at the handsome little man. Perhaps he will fall off! Ai Ya! They all smile. Look, the blue-eyed ones smile. Aren't they funny?"

Children race to keep along side us, and farmers straighten their backs and twist their necks to watch us pass on the "Foreign-make-yourself-go-car," as they call our bicycles. We ride on the mud embankments between rice paddies or on the dusty lanes between villages. Now and then we have seen small stone and earth-covered structures. They are Japanese-built pill boxes which the Chinese will no doubt find some use for!

Teaching at Ginling is going well. My students are adorable. Their bad habits are legion after a whole year without any teacher, but we are doing what we can. They want to learn Western style of voice training, but getting rid of their metallic shrillness is work. When they finally relax, their voices are lovely. The campus is gorgeous, though most buildings are shabby from neglect during the war years.

Ginling College Seniors

Gao Seu Tsung

Hwang You Lien

Judy and Tom

Tom Cowles
Nanking, 1947

Tom

Mother and children begging in the street

They are in the classic winged-roof style, and should be brightly painted, but now are pale reflections of their former beauty.

Just got back from a fun bike trip past a lot of Chinese shops. We stopped to visit our Suan T'ang Church and school over in a miserable section of the city. Children of all ages surrounded us, and crowded close about our knees. My big white shoes caused lots of snickers. Chinese women's feet are tiny, so mine look like gunboats to them. They like my blond hair, though.

Chinese shops are a little like California fruit stands in that they are all open at the front. When we stop anywhere we leave our bikes at the curb. Immediately one crowd forms around the bike, while another follows us and presses close to hear and see all the funny things we say and do. There are very few bicycles, so people are nearly as fascinated by them as by us.

Once in a while, things get more than a little out of hand. The other day I decided to put Judy in her carriage and go for a walk down our street. Some little boys decided to tease me by getting down on all fours to block the carriage wheels. Then they decided to toss orange peels into the carriage. I tried to smile and keep going, but when more and more had gathered, adults as well as children, I began to be uneasy. I took carriage and all into a shop, thinking that if we were out of sight they would lose interest and leave.

Wrong! More and more crowded up until there was a small mob out there. There was nothing to do but face them and turn towards home as fast as possible. They allowed me to leave the store, but started tossing pebbles from the street into Judy's carriage. I moved as fast as I could, trying not to look as scared as I felt. They all moved right along with me. At last I reached the Methodist Compound. Luckily a servant was out in front. He opened the gates, shooed me inside, and closed them behind us. A few (children mostly) climbed the wall, but most left in a few minutes. I won't be repeating that mistake any time soon!

This China! It is sometimes too wild to believe. A man comes to our door and politely requests money to support his profession. What is it? Beating a stick on a hollow wooden object to frighten "small thieves" away from other people's walls. It is extortion, pure and simple, yet is a recognized and legitimate part of life here. Once a year, too, the “King of Thieves” comes around for his payoff. We had an epidemic of thieves here two weeks ago. Then we told the man about it, his answer was: “That was before you paid me!”

A few days ago I had seven teeth filled by the US Army dentist. I had made an appointment for a later date, but his orders to return to America came through suddenly, so he called me over to finish up before he left. I kidded him about his roughness, and said he’d better brush up on how to handle wealthy widows before returning to Stateside civilian practice. He answered that I had the only female jaw he had looked into except for Madame Chiangs. He added that she was a sissy, and yelled all through her appointment!

LIFE AND DEATH IN NANKING

Nanking, China
March 31, 1947

Spring is here. Trees are fully leafed out, grass is greening and flowers are beginning to show color. People on the street look much thinner, because they have shed their padded winter garments. There is a high, thin flute sound in the air coming from pigeons with little whistles fastened to their legs.

Of forty missionaries in Nanking, eight are Presbyterian. We rarely see any of the reputed five hundred Americans here. American Army Advisory Group men live together on the other side of town. Embassy folk are concentrated on Embassy Row. Young American women are a rarity. Children, likewise. In all of Nanking, there are only forty of them.

Some older missionary children are in school in Shanghai. There is a Sunday School which meets at the American grade school. About thirty-four attend. Tom goes. It is the high point of his week.

You asked about the cleanliness of the students who come into our house. It is hard to generalize. Some are, many, perhaps most, are not. How can they be when their homes are so filthy? A Harvard fellow studying at Nanking University is living with a family of one of the professors (husband and wife both university graduates). They empty tea grounds, bones and scraps on the floor around the table and on the table itself, and do other things that would horrify us. STANDARDS are so different here. My Ginling girls are way above average in personal cleanliness. It is difficult for anyone to keep clean in Nanking. When there is no mud, there are clouds of dust. I have never seen such dust.

Saturday we and three friends hired a horse and carriage and went to the Ming tombs for a picnic. We ate canned Vienna sausages (in lieu of wieners) between slices of bread and butter, potato salad, tangerines and bananas, chocolate chip cookies (using UNRRA butterscotch pudding powder instead of sugar), cocoa for the kids, coffee for us. We always take a bottle of alcohol and cotton with which hands must be carefully washed before we eat.

We sat on a hill above a farm. Before we had been there fifteen minutes the Chinese people began to gather. Fifteen of them stood through our whole meal, watching and commenting on everything. They weren't hungry: some of them were eating their own lunch while they watched us. Just curious. It is a strain never to be alone. There are good reasons for compound walls, I've found.

Nanking, China
April 3, 1947

This morning I went to Ginling, taught from eight until eleven-thirty and sang at their Chapel services. Tonight I have to sing at two communion services at Twinem Chapel.

Yesterday afternoon we took our regular two-hour bike ride and sight-seeing trip. As usual, each time we stopped we were surrounded. One time we passed about twenty-five men pulling a concrete roller to level the road. When they saw me, they all STOPPED PULLING TO LAUGH. I had my hair up in a bandana, as I had washed it, and they thought it was another version of foreign women's hats. I just grinned and rode on.

We just received a letter from a student who called here yesterday afternoon. With his friend he fooled around twenty minutes without saying anything in particular. Ben made a date with the friend who said he "had some problems to discuss." In this letter the boy says that Ben "ordered him to go." Obviously, Ben did nothing of the kind, but the fact that this student thought he did shows how barriers of customs and language can lead to serious misunderstandings.

Students right now are in a hypersensitive, inflammable state. That's how the student demonstrations are fanned so quickly into being.

Remember our rats? We're having a terrible time getting rid of them. Two nights ago we caught a big one in Judy's room, not four feet from her bed. One night Ben and a visiting friend spent several hours up in the third floor chasing rats with baseball bats. They got six! There are three small bedrooms up there which, when we arrived, still had women's names on the doors, so we have a pretty good idea what the Japanese General who lived here was using them for.

PEGGY KORDICK

Nanking, China
April 9, 1947

Yesterday we had a lot of excitement. There is a city bus stop immediately in front of our gate and another across the street in front of Ming Te Middle School gate. When I returned from Ginling at about noon, several buses were stopped here, and a crowd was milling around. Our cook told me a fight was going on. Our coolie was holding our bug-eyed Tom right in the center of things, so I brought Tom inside our compound and took him to our second-floor windows to watch. (These windows are just above the street.)

Before long, real trouble started. Thank goodness I hadn't returned any later. I'd have walked right into it! Supposedly, the trouble was between University of Political Science students (a government school) and the bus drivers over the drivers' refusal to sell one student a half-fare ticket. There must have been more than that behind it.

A real riot developed, surging back and forth, always right in front of our house. The civilian and military police both came, and by one-thirty things were relatively quiet, although a mob of people remained. Dr. Mills barred our gates and advised us to keep out of sight, because in times of violence, foreigners traditionally become targets.

We thought it was dying down, but just at three a new crowd of students arrived, armed with clubs. They beat people and threw their clubs (a few landed in our yard), then they proceeded to break all the windows in the one bus which was left standing at our bus stop. I didn't see all that happened then, but the cook said a military policeman was clubbed unconscious during the brawl which followed. Soon twenty or more civilian and military police arrived, and with bayonets slowly stopped the violence and sent the onlookers about their business. The crippled bus was towed away. By nightfall, all was peaceful. But what a day!

All that afternoon the Executive Committee of Presbytery was meeting in our house. Also, from one-thirty to three-thirty I was having a Chinese lesson. My teacher remarked that foreigners think it laughable that Chinese should do such things. I said no, only that it is a great pity.

By the way, Miss Stella Graves, the present head of the music department at Ginling, has asked me to sing three of her recently published Min River Boat Songs as her part of the faculty recital on May 3. These beautiful songs are Chinese folk tunes, collected by Malcolm Farley and harmonized by Miss Graves. In addition, I'll have to do a ten minute program of my own.

PEGGY KORDICK

Nanking, China
Sunday, April 20, 1947

Honestly, the weeks slip by so swiftly that it is beyond belief that two of them have passed since I last wrote. The student riot I was talking about then was serious, and has had many repercussions. The high school most mixed up in it has been told no Nanking University or college will accept its graduated students in the fall.

Saturday we went biking and took Tom to see the foreign cemetery. It is a serenely beautiful spot inside Nanking's wall, yet appears to be in the country. There is a low wall around it, and there are about fifty tombstones, now grass covered and ill-kempt. It was startling to find Dr. Mills there, as we hadn't known he meant to go there, too. A lot of tiny markers bear witness to the heavy toll among children. One I noticed read: "Nov. 15, Dec. 16, 1916."

We walked around the cemetery wall and climbed up on the city wall directly behind it. From that vantage-point, we could look straight down into the grass-hut village below and see the river and the country beyond. You cannot imagine how these people live. We counted fifty-six huts in an area smaller than our compound. Tiny children were running about stark naked, playing in the carefree way of children, in such surroundings. Everywhere filth, and everywhere humanity.

Sunday noon we had Dr. Chester Miao and Sally Wiley as guests for lunch and Dr. Rolla Ram and Miss Sarah Chakko came for dinner. The latter two are on a goodwill tour through China from India. People here are so intense about India's politics that these two have complained of having little or no opportunity to speak with Chinese friends about spiritual matters. Hence, we asked ten Chinese pastors and lay leaders and professors from the seminary over after dinner to talk with the Indians.

Our servants were so unabashedly curious at Miss Chakko's flowing Indian robes and Dr. Ram's strange leggings that I was embarrassed. It got worse. Tom, who had asked to see Miss Chakko in his bedroom as his price for good behavior, asked her where she got her "funny face."

She is a remarkable woman. Later at the table she told us about it, chuckling and describing it as "delicious." Tom told me the next morning she had said she was born with it and it "just grew on her," No doubt he was referring to her dark skin and meant no harm, but I had a chat with him about rudeness.

Friday evening at six Ben took me with him to his regular weekly lecture on "Christianity and Democracy" at the Central Political Science Academy, a Kuomintang-sponsored university of two thousand students, a few blocks from our house. We biked over cobblestone, rutted roads, only to find that we were an hour early. The main part of Nanking went on what they call Sunlight Savings Time on April 15, but this school had not.

One student asked us to wait in his room, and led us to it. It was freezing cold, bleak, a small square space whose walls did not reach to the sloping ceiling. Noises came from everywhere at once. The rooms are more spartan than our Army barracks, and house from four to six students each. The only similarity to American College boys' rooms was the "pin-up-girl" pictures (American) on the wall. There were few books, no radios, no rugs on the floor, and the beds had no mattresses, only quilts.

Very few of those students are Christians, but Ben is getting quite a following over there. After his hour and one-half speech, imagine my chagrin to be informed that they expected a speech from me as well. I gave a two minute pep talk, and got by. When we got home at eight-thirty, there stood the cook, the amah, the cook's son, the amah's nephew, our coolie, and little Tom, all lined up in the dusk in front of our gate. I never found out why.

Saturday, at three, I sang for a one-year anniversary celebration held at the YWCA. Among others there, I was surprised to see Ambassador Stuart and a great many Chinese and European diplomats. The YW is pioneering in mother and child care, craft work, and doing an excellent job. It was great to see it being recognized by so many of the foreign community. I have been helping out there whenever I can find the time.

Immediately after the Y affair, I took a rickshaw home to change clothes, as it was fearfully hot, and to give orders for the children's care while I was gone again. Off to the American Embassy where Dr. Stuart was giving a garden tea to acquaint the various categories of Americans with one another, and to introduce to the American community the dozens of Army wives who had just arrived.

Sunday morning I taught a Bible class, English, of non-Christian high school boys at Han Chung.' At ten thirty I took Tom to the American Sunday School at Hillcrest Elementary School. There I led the singing and helped a little with Tom's class. There is no Chinese Sunday School in the city that our children can attend.

In fact, religious education is the weakest link in the work here. It has always been. The type of Christianity found in churches here would often be hard to recognize. The Devil is much more real and vividly portrayed than either a loving Heavenly Father or a compassionate Jesus. They have pictures of Hell in the Sunday School rooms that would scare anyone. Why? I don't pretend to know.

Just as Chinese with little knowledge of English are teaching English everywhere here, so Bible women and even pastors who don't even understand Christianity have tried to force converts and scare people into being "saved" (from Hell, but certainly not TO anything). A formidable state of ignorance exists even in the church itself. At times we feel we are doing nothing out here. Other times, we feel all our efforts are being poured down the drain, but always underneath is that steady voice which demands that we stay, and assures us this is the place we must be.

Most of my teaching at present is in English, but all committee meetings and other affairs are entirely in Chinese. I have started studying with a tutor two hours every afternoon. To my great relief, I am fast improving. My slowness in the language has been a barrier ever since I came. Now I can converse with more and more ease.

Tom is growing up. He is trying more and more to speak Chinese, and does much better at it every day. The servants are delighted, and teach him as much as they can. He is very self-important these days, and solemnly urges us to hurry through breakfast because his teacher is coming(!) or he "Got to teach my Bible class."

Nanking, China
May 2, 1947

Oh, what a long time it has been since we sailed on December 9! We have literally stepped into another world, and that pleasant, easy (though rushed) pattern of days in Berkeley is already relegated to the status of daydream, or at least reverie. Five months? Five decades!

The gray and yellow ugliness of winter has pretty much been replaced by greenness this spring, but the careworn and haggard faces, the grime, poverty and cruelty are very much still here.

About seven-thirty each evening Tom's pajama clad figure may be seen in his window as he stares with great absorption at the scene below. American trucks (Chinese owned and driven), buses, jeeps and autos roar past with great blaring of horns or claxons in a cloud of stinging, yellow dust. Simultaneously, a gaggle of geese and perhaps a herd of black pigs will go honking and squealing past, urged along by whips and kicks from the rear. Rickshaws, pedicabs, bicycles, wheelbarrows (with excruciating squeaks), and all sorts of push carts and horse carriages loaded until the axles groan and crack and the poor, emaciated horses sweat and steam, these are all part of the daily panorama. And then there are tiny children, filthy, ragged, but invariably shiny-eyed. This, even when their little bodies are twisted and swollen with disease.

The roads are incredibly awful. Ruts, jagged rocks, and deep holes are accepted as a matter of course. There is one, long, macadamized street at the city's heart, but all others are worse than would be found in the poorest town at home, and this is China's capital!

Last night was the Ginling faculty recital. The place was jammed. Extra seats had been added in aisles and across both front and back, since the music building only holds fifteen hundred people. A funny sidelight: the weather has been very cold, and, as I've had a sore throat and cough, I decided to wear something warmer than just the sleeveless black evening gown. I cunningly donned first a long-sleeved sweater, then a blue, long-sleeved China silk blouse, and then the dress. The effect wasn't too bad, but imagine how like a sissy I felt to find ALL the other teachers in Chinese formal (sleeveless) gowns. Oh well, live and learn!

This next week, due to poor coordination between various mission agencies, we will have a giant crowd around here. The Kiangan Synod meets for the first time in ten years; the Chinese Medical Association, just getting organized, is having its first big gathering; there is a Preaching Mission to Young People which involves seven speakers from outside Nanking, and five universities and six middle schools—all these this week!

With housing scarce to none, there's a problem. We will house twelve of the men of Synod from Tuesday until the following Monday. We'll have three of them in the third floor guest room, two in the study, two in the second floor guest room, and the rest in the Little House, as we call the converted garage. Of the twelve, eight are foreigners and four are Chinese. Meals (Chinese of course) are to be pretty much provided by the host church, which is Han Chung. We will serve them breakfasts and dinner whenever their tummies can't take Chinese food twice a day.

This morning I started teaching an English class on the life of Jesus to twenty four senior girls from Ming Deh High School across the street. As I have observed them coming and going to school I have wished there was some way to know them. Last week after the principal asked me to sing for a student assembly, a request came for my help.

Things in China seem more in a turmoil than ever. The students are like tinder boxes. Any real or imagined incident sets off a riot. The war goes on and on and no one can tell what is happening. Inflation has gotten out of control: Prices have doubled again this week. The Communists are fighting with as much strength as ever. Last week they made gains fifty miles from Nanking!

Nanking, China
May 27, 1947

Right now I'm writing from bed. Nothing serious, just a tummy upset. Dysentery is so common here that there seems to be no one who escapes it. Since I have cleaned up the kitchen and laundry techniques, we suffer about as little as anyone from it, but an upset now and then cannot be avoided when the whole rest of China has it!

Amah is in Judy's room giving her "hsi tsao" (a bath). I did that myself until two weeks ago, but it's the one part of the day's duties amah really enjoys, so I've let her take over. She's a fine person and her years of work for various missionary families seem not to have destroyed her confidence in them. She has raised three or four adopted children, and is now in the process of helping support the subsequent grandchildren. She is devoted to Judy, and cooperates admirably with Tom, though his deviltry threatens to turn her graying hair pure white!

My two prima donnas at Ginling gave their senior recitals on successive nights this past week. They wore white formal gowns of Chinese brocaded silk, and absolutely sparkled. An interesting sidelight: on the program with one student, Miss Gao, was Miss Shen, daughter of Bishop Shen of Shanghai. Miss Gao is from Peking, from a wealthy family, so she had a gorgeous dress to wear.

Miss Shen was not to be outshown. (She is really the prettier of the two). Her family could not afford the silk for a dress at today's exorbitant prices, so she and her mother cut up a quilt protector which was found in a family trunk, and had a dress of prewar silk as beautiful as any girl could wish for. Shades of Scarlett O'Hara! Chinese formal gowns are cut just like their street dresses, except that they are sleeveless and ankle-length.

The student riots you have been hearing about are serious and have dangerous implications. The government falsifies all reports of such things, so it is necessary to talk to eyewitnesses to make sure you are hearing the truth. That we have done, and their reports of the May 20th riot are frightening.

The police and government plainclothesmen used unbelievable brutality, wielding nail studded clubs, whips, and ropes to try to end the demonstration. Later they said that the students had done the damage, and that the whole affair was Communist inspired. No doubt the Communists have a hand in it somewhere, but to charge it totally to them and to disregard the other equally important elements is absolute blindness. The students ARE hungry, the government is wasting money, the civil war SHOULD be stopped, and the people feel these things deeply.

The government misses the boat when it uses violence to suppress such genuine expressions of the public mind and will. We are all fearful of what will occur on June second, the day set for a general demonstration all over China. The stage is set for slaughter. Students and government alike are in an ugly mood. Time will tell which side wins.

Meanwhile, our vacation plans are taking shape. We plan to leave here July fourteenth and stay in the mountains of Kuling until September first. We had not planned to go, thinking we could not afford it, but the older missionaries said we could not afford not to. The Jones have secured a house from their Methodist group which is large enough to share. Life will be rough, but, we hope, restful and fun.

There will be no electricity, running water, or furniture, There will be mountains, coolness, places to swim and hike, and a certain delicious distance from crowds. We will leave here at four a.m. by boat up the Yangtze River, and will travel two days to Kiukiang. From there we are to be hauled by truck to the foot of the mountain where "carriers" tote us the rest of the way. Obviously, this means a minimum of supplies and equipment. The house itself is rumored to be comfortable, airy, and clean. (I'll believe that when I see it.) Judy will probably be walking by the time we go, so she'll be a problem, but we're taking our cook and the Jones' amah, so it won't be too bad.

Yesterday we pedaled out to the Foreign Cemetery for the Memorial Day service. Dr. Stuart spoke. Last evening I entertained all six senior music students and seven teachers from Ginling at dinner. We had ice cream from our refrigerator. They loved it!

Wednesday night we were entertained by the Beals. He is a *Time* man loaned by the U.S. government to the Chinese government as an advisor. He is the son of missionaries to India. Also there were Fred and Violet Gruen. He is the *Time* correspondent for Nanking. His story on Chen Li Fu was in this week's *Time*, but he hadn't seen it yet, so was hoping it had been accurately printed. He is brilliant. The evening was fascinating, as we compared impressions of what is going on in China right now. The Beals' little girl, Caroline, is Tom's age and comes over here to play quite frequently.

Nanking, China
June 9, 1947

This is a wonderful day for work indoors. The wind is blowing hard, and there are occasional hard downpours of rain. Tom and Judy are playing with building blocks (Tom is building, Judy is sabotaging!).

Last week we hit a peak in absolute discouragement. This job is impossible! No one knows what we are here to do, and when we try to find out for ourselves we bat our heads against a stone wall. The mission personnel here are a discouraging lot. The older ones "have seen it all before," and fail to recognize that China's travail of today requires more effort and FASTER than what they have known in the past.

If they see you have any spirit or any initiative, the idea is to crush it as fast as possible, so you'll be apathetic like the rest. Our hands and feet and mouths are bound by rules and traditions until initiative and even thought becomes too wearisome to trouble with. There are no middle people to bridge the gap between the old missionaries and our younger group. There are the "first timers" and those who have been here off and on for forty years, but few, practically none, between. In solving problems, which, because of the times, requires a new approach, we're at an impasse.

The Chinese, too, contribute to frustration more often than joy or hope. They use us for what they can get out of us, but refuse to take responsibility, and the games they play with finances leave us reeling. Those who really understand Christianity are so terribly few. Those who use it for their own advancement are so many. At every point we are shackled by lack of personnel and money and other more insidious obstacles understood only by the Chinese themselves.

Across the street is Ming Deh Middle School for Girls. It was founded some sixty years ago by our mission, and now, in spite of the war's destruction, flourishing. Two thousand girls are enrolled, but only three girls come to the Han Chung Church young people's group and not more than six attend church! Something wrong? Surely. But what? The answer to that one is not easy, but we're trying to find it.

The same family that controls the school has the pastor of the church under its thumb, so you would think the school would support the church, wouldn't you? Since they DON'T, you can see the complexity of the problem. Yesterday, in talking it over with some of the older mission people, they said it would work itself out. Perhaps. But what makes me sleepless is this generation of girls passing through the school completely apart from the church. How to reach them?

The political picture looks blacker all the time. Hardly anyone thinks this government can last out the year. If the Communists take over, we'll certainly have to leave. Still, no one knows, and few even guess what lies ahead.

Nanking, China
June 13, 1947

We're still planning to go to Kuling, though shouldn't be surprised if we'll be blocked the last minute by Communists. Several of our friends have had recent encounters with them and have lost EVERYTHING. One, Norman McKenzie, a Canadian, is in their hands now, his wife Dottie and son Ian having escaped to temporary safety. We've heard from Peking that they are all slowed down by the Communist shadow around them. Peking has for some time been completely surrounded.

Still, our Army people are planning vacations in Kuling this summer (they go by air), so the enigma of danger vs. no danger we are all living in!

We often kid each other about how the Communists will like our stove, refrigerator, etc., and what color they would like us to paint our bedroom. It's a crazy feeling; not too pleasant.

What a blessing our refrigerator is in this scalding heat. Ice, ice cream, and refrigeration for meats is a godsend. Also, the washer is at last being used. It is in the second floor bathroom, and amah and I use it two or three times a week. If you could see the water she usually "rinses" clothes in and smell the clothes when she's brought them in, you'd know why I'm so thankful to get them clean. Amahs beat the clothes, rub bar soap into them, twist them hard, then hang them where clouds of dust roll.

Nanking, China
June 16, 1947

Last evening we had dinner at the home of General Hwang. Other guests were General Lee and his wife and Mr. and Mrs. Chen. Chen is soon to leave for Ecuador, where he will be consul. After a banquet, they showed us the American movie *Magnificent Doll*, plus newsreels showing President Truman giving the Greece/Turkey speech in Congress and elephants playing volleyball in the zoo. I don't know where they got it, but it was fun seeing it, although the mosquitoes were so bad I was one big, red lump when we got home.

We are sleeping under mosquito netting all of the time now. Ours looks like a canopy. It is hung from a circular wooden frame about six feet above the bed to allow as much breeze as possible. Tom sleeps in a hospital bed with steel poles at head and foot to support his net. Judy's just falls down over her crib. Tom says: "She looks like a lion in a cage."

PEGGY KORDICK

Kulling, China
July 18, 1947

You would love it here. On July 6th we came by way of Kiukiang on a Yangtze River steamer in a reasonable degree of comfort. About the first of June the Yangtze valley settles down to a torridly steamy summer, and stays that way well into October as a rule. The kids had broken out into severe cases of prickly heat like nothing I've seen before. Great yellow topped red blisters all over faces, necks, shoulders, and tummies. The coolness here is healing them.

The evening of the second day we pulled into Kiukiang and piled off. I mean PILED. We had stacks of heavy baggage, as we had to bring foodstuffs and some household equipment. After the fellows unloaded this mountain of stuff, we two gals and our kids perched on it while they went off to bargain for a truck to haul it to the foot of the mountain.

Chinese people are fascinated by everything we do, so it wasn't long before seventy five or so had gathered in a circle around us for a closer look. There they stayed until we left. Not only that, but the ship remained at the pier, and people were jammed at the rail of all four decks just staring at us without moving. We have to act as though they aren't there, stare over their heads, and pretend indifference. Even Tom has become calloused to it, but now and then I find him making faces or funny noises to while away the time. If there's no barrier, we get squashed!

We were too late that night, and it rained next day, so we didn't go up the mountain until the day after. We spent that night in a Methodist mission. When we were ready to go we took a truck from Kiukiang to the foot of the mountain. From there we were carried up a steep path by bearers with sedan chairs These are very light, made of bamboo, two long poles with a basket like seat secured to the middle. To hire them we had to bargain loud and long. Hordes of steaming, dirty coolies push and pull at you and your stuff, yelling at the top of their lungs to try to intimidate you into hiring them.

The din, heat, and confusion are unbelievable! I finally just stopped in my tracks and screamed "SHUT UP AND GET OUT!" in English, and they scattered, but were soon back again. Martha got so mad she finally socked one fellow. They just drive you NUTS.

Kuling was formerly a virtual foreign colony, but during the war many Chinese moved in, so there is a more normal balance now. Many of the lovely houses were burned and otherwise destroyed. The valley we look down on is called Methodist Valley, since all of the twenty or so houses belong to the Methodists. We are horning in by sharing a Swiss chalet type duplex with the Tracey Jones. It is at the top of one ridge.

Directly below me a gang of coolies is working to restore the swimming pool to usable condition. Water is piped from higher up the mountain by way of bamboo pipes. The first Chinese contractor hired delivered the pipes all right, but after he collected his money and left, it was discovered that the bamboo had not been hollowed out! Ah, gullibility!

A little further down from us is a sprawling, roofless shambles of what once must have been a beautiful house. Red and gray tiled rooftops dot the trees in the distance until the eye reaches the smooth, rolling edges of the ranges beyond this one. The white expanse of Chiang Kai Shek's summer residence looms among the trees on a far away hill.

In Nanking we were always aware of ugliness and hatred of us very close to the surface. Even up here guards poke loaded rifles in our stomachs when we go on hikes or just walk from here to there. They demand our passports and lecture us surlily on the fact that the "Wai Kuo Jen" (foreigners) do not run China now! There are both military and civilian police all over these mountains.

We have to be very careful. The Chinese are teetering between dependence on and a bitter resentment of America. Here, as in Nanking, we are alternately slapped on the back and kicked in the pants.

Kuling, China
August 3, 1947

We are still in Kulling, having a GLORIOUS time. A full two-month vacation is a luxury we'll not often enjoy, but this year we are reveling in it. Those who have just arrived up here from various points up and down the Yangtze report that it is the most merciless heat in years. Several families have reported children BEDFAST with prickly heat. Can you imagine? The humidity is unbearable. I said it could not be worse than Washington, D.C., but, oh, how wrong I was. It will still be hot through September, so we'll have one month to stand after our return, but our lazy, cool days up here should put us into good shape.

The other night we were sitting in the main room playing games by lantern light when there was a loud yell from our Judy. I rushed into her room with a flashlight, and found her sitting up in bed, her eyes about to pop out of her head. She stopped wailing at once, and started very earnestly to describe what had happened, gesturing and pointing with her fat, little arms, and frowning and scolding in the funniest and most fluent gibberish you ever heard.

After one look at her blanket, I caught on. A RAT had been on her bed! I took her out in the other room, where she continued to gesture and describe her horrible experience with a pop-eyed earnestness that was too comical for words. The following night we caught the rat in a trap.

Last night we returned home after a walk to find Judy uncovered, and sleeping with only a diaper on. When we questioned Tom later, he said, "A'nake came in and took her nightie off."

"But how, Tom?"

"Wiss his hands."

"But snakes don't HAVE hands, Tom."

"This was a big, funny 'nake wiss hands. It was black and white and red."

"But how could it reach her?"

"It stood on his feets—dis funny 'nake had feets, too."

That's his story, and he doesn't change it. We said we found out the nake's name—T. Kendall 'Nake, and he turned his head to hide his smile.

Friday we took a long hike to a place called "Paradise Pools." It is well named, for though we were hot and nearly exhausted when we got there, one foot in that crystal clear cold water made us like new. There are three pools with a rocky climb between them. All are about two hundred feet across. The water drops about seventy feet over the rocks into the highest one, passes over and under huge boulders, and drops about fifty feet into the second, then rushes down about three hundred yards to the third. There are redwood trees in groves surrounding the pools.

We swam in two of the pools. There is a swimming pool near our house in Methodist Valley, but every time there is a rain, mud washes in from the mountains above, and it must be drained, cleaned, refilled and chlorinated: a painful, exasperating process.

PEGGY KORDICK

Letter from Tom to Grandpa
Kuling, China
August 25, 1947

I am sick today. I am playing with pretty 'poons mommie gave me with long handles on them. When we go 'wimming we take a pillow and we 'wim, It's COLD. Daddy just came home. He and Uncle Tracey been playin' tennis ebry day. Grarnpah and Grahmah, I hab some books. Tell Grampaw and Grammaw dev nub (love) me and dare good to me and dey sent me sings and I nub dem so much. Mommie, where's Grawmaw and Grampa and Jonn? Where are dey? Do dey nib in Berkeley? No, dey came to Berkeley and took us to free Ribbers. I hab a feever today. When will I be well? Write de new shoes you bought, mommie. How nong are dem? Dey're Chinese tennis shoes. Dey are brown. When we get back to Manking we'll see Hsiao Mei Mei. Tell dem Plummer Mills flew to 'merica in an airplane. Is dere a packudge for us in Nanking?

Mommie, de next day if we see an ice cream cone truck could you ask de man to gib me one of dose kind of ice cream suckers? But dey don't hab dose in China, do dey? My baby sister is nearning to walk. She nooks funny. We ate cereal for breakfast, also biscuits and egg. Ask dem about Free Bibbers. Where are dey? Does Grawmnaw hab any shickens now? Tell dem if I can find some eggs and make green pudding.

My pail's broken. Isn't dat too bad? Grampaw, hab you 'membered dat I fell in de ribber? I fell in de pool at Kuling, grawrnnaw. One girl in a red bathing suit pulled me out.

Are you mad at me 'cause I felled in? Do you know what we had on Sunday morning in Nanking? Pancakes! An' w'en de Han Chung Church ding bell rings, dat means we put on a red beanie hat and den we go to Sunny Schoo'.

Beggars are naughty, aren't dey? When a rickshot man brings us home in a rickshot, we see all dose men in brown coats, and dey nook funny. Tell Grawmpaw Judy Jones has a new house in Manking. I nike Chinese food. It's good, and I eat it and Judy Jones eats it with shopsticks. We used to eat it in Nanking, and our cook makes it' up here, too! Isn' dat berry, berry funny?

Could I write netters when I hab a missionary (stationary) and get to be a big daddy? Sometimes the hsien ping (military police) stop us and stick a gun in him. Dey shoot lions and frees, but not people, because Jesus and God don't take guns, so we don't like guns to Sunny 'coo', do we?

God paintses de sunset, doesn't he, mama? Mama, how did Bradley get (become) a dead boy? I'm tired now from writing dis netter. Tell den too bad, too bad, too BAD. Betty Ann gotses two grawmpaws and two grawmmaws, but I got on'y one grawmpaw and on'y one grawmmaw. I tired now, so tell dem I goin' to sleep.

Nanking again
September 9, 1947

The last couple of weeks at Kuling disappeared in no time. The weather was exquisite, and we hated to leave. Tom had a mysterious low-grade fever for a week, which the doctor finally diagnosed as malaria. He wasn't sick; his only trial was being kept in bed.

There had been lots of soldiers being moved down river, so transportation was uncertain. Sunday, September 1st, when we heard of a large rice-freighter going straight to Nanking, we hastily packed up and hurried down the mountain. On the way down the narrow path, we encountered a beautiful chair being borne by rich blue-silk-clad coolies. The lady inside the chair leaned forward and looked so intently at me that I inadvertently smiled at her...before I realized with a shock who she was...Madame Chiang!

She returned my smile instantly, and graciously bowed. In another instant her chair had passed, and I was looking into the face of the Generalissimo, whose chair was directly behind his wife's. The path is so narrow that it barely affords space for two chairs to pass, so it would have been possible to reach out to touch either of them. Except that I'd have most likely been shot by one or all of the immense number of military guard following them. It was a spectacle. There were dozens of dignitaries in chairs immediately following them, and, of course, the guard.

Tom was funny. I told him the reason I was so excited was that that was the most important man in China. I guess I didn't explain which man, because, a little further down we encountered a poor, tired, hot coolie in the lovely dark blue silk who must have dropped behind from fatigue. Tom said: "Oh, look, mommie! There's another important, pretty man!" (Tom and I shared a chair).

We spent the night in Kiukiang again, and found out with a bang about the terrible heat we had been missing all summer. Tuesday morning at seven we were on the Yangtze River boat ready to go. It didn't sail until ten-thirty. The trip was not nearly as hot as we had anticipated, clouds and a strong wind kept us from feeling the sun's fiercest rays.

By eight-thirty the following morning we had reached Nanking, and the struggle to get our baggage unsnarled was fully under way. Dr. Trimmer was at the wharf to meet us in the hospital ambulance, since his wife and daughter were on the same boat. He piled all the women and children in and drove us straight home. The poor men had to stay in the steaming heat among sweating, yelling coolies, getting a truck to bring our stuff home.

How cool, clean, and quiet our house seemed after the summer's makeshifts and the travel confusion! The servants weren't expecting us for another week, but the place was superbly clean, and even the yard looked trimmed and lovely.

They all raved over the fatness of the children and Judy's ability to walk. They came running to Tom's room on the second floor to see her do it! Tom, of course, rushed from one place to another exclaiming over nearly-forgotten treasures, while Judy staggered and plunked her unsteady way through the unaccustomed expanse of space.

Of course, our gregarious amah had filled her house with her leech-like relatives. I counted at least ten strange faces. She had also acquired at least seven new chickens. All of this will be dealt with in due time, but just now we're too pleased to be home to disturb it with squabbles.

In your letter you asked whether we weren't really more often up than down. Oh, yes, we surely are! A great burden has been rolled off me, too, for now, since vacation, I suddenly find myself really deep-down loving China. Things which irritated and discouraged me before, do not bother now. What a relief it is. At last, I'm beginning to feel at home here.

Life goes on. A few minutes ago a man came in great distress to beg me to write a letter to try to get his child admitted quickly to the hospital as the child is suddenly deathly ill, and the man is desperate. I did, of course. Yesterday afternoon I'd just returned by ricksha from the bank, when I met a Chinese Brigadier General at our gate who implored me to teach him English.

Footnote added the following Wednesday:

This was signed, sealed and addressed, but not mailed, so, since I'm so upset, I decided to add another page. This morning, as I was dressing and looking out our second-floor bedroom window towards

Han Chung Church, I noticed that all who passed one corner of our wall were showing strange reactions to what they saw out there. Some stopped and stared, others, men and women as well as children, clapped one hand over mouth and nose, the other over their eyes, and ran past.

Suspicious, I went outside our gate to see. Sure enough, down the alley a little way, between our house and the church, was the body of a dead child, about six years old, wrapped in the square, straw mat the Chinese use in summer to sleep on. The pathetic little shaven head was projecting, unprotected, on the mud.

Shaken, I hurried in and told the cook to go call the police or whatever else needed to be done. Foreigners do not meddle in such events. The cook observed that though it was against our wall, it was also in the lane used by Ming Deh school children, so probably Ming Deh would do something about it. It is now eight hours later, and the little body still lies there. The police know it. I saw them looking at it.

Many hundreds of people have passed by, some in horror, some in fear, some showing only curiosity. But NO ONE HELPS. If it died of some contagious disease, so much the worse for passersby, but still no one moves it. I have tried all day to put the thoughts of it from me, but I cannot. All I can think is that yesterday some mother had her child with her and could take care of it. In the night it left her, and in her sorrow she still had to subject the precious little body to this indignity.

This has happened here before. Before I came, the men who were cleaning up the long neglected yard around this house found the bodies of five babies hidden in the tall grass and weeds. They had been shoved over our wall, because they were found right next to it.

Chinese callousness to this kind of thing is perhaps better in some ways. It happens so often to them. Perhaps some day I, too, will learn to "take it in stride." But, oh, what a weight on one's heart! We need God in so many ways.

LIFE AND DEATH IN NANKING

Nanking, China
September 27, 1947
7:30 PM

What happened to the abandoned dead baby? Someone finally came and hauled the body away on a wheelbarrow late that afternoon. The little boy whose father asked me to write a letter to the hospital for him later died in the hospital. You can imagine our emotions when yesterday the father came bringing a live chicken, a basket of pears, and one of bananas and two boxed of moon cakes as a "gratitude offering." To have refused him would have been unheard of according to Chinese custom, yet how sad to accept!

This is the Moon Festival season, and there are lots of parades of pilgrims to the temples passing our house on Moh Tsou Lu. The paper banners and lanterns are very colorful. The youngsters and I make a dash for the windows whenever we hear the deep-toned gongs and clanging cymbals that signal their approach. More obnoxious, however, are the activities of the Buddhist priests next door who start about eight p.m. to rattle gongs and beat their "jigaboo" rhythms on hard drums. What a racket! It's like having your window open on a hot dance band playing full blast until late at night. How the servants sleep I don't know.

My personal biggest news is really big. At the meeting of the International Women's Club on September 23, (the first of this season) we had as our speaker Madame Chiang Kai Shek. I was the soloist! Yes, really! I've never been so nervous!

All the know-it-alls (we've been in China thirty years, my child) said she would sweep in just in time for her address and sweep out again when finished. To my personal satisfaction she came early for tea, went with the crowd into the program hall, heard me sing "Snow" and the "Glory Road," spoke (in English of course), heard my pal Mrs. Feng of Ginling play two numbers, and then left with the rest of us.

She is really very beautiful gracious and most markedly graceful. Her talk was to the point, frank and brief, but thorough. The sparkling charm for which she is noted was totally absent. She seems rather quiet, tired, preoccupied in repose, and somewhat severe and almost defiant while talking. Of course the pending U.S. loan hung in the air and her attitude betrayed the serious plight of Chiang's government. She was dressed in a gray and lavender flowered Chinese gown and wore gray suede Western-style pumps. Her voice and manner are queenly. She is truly a commanding presence. All of the Embassy and Army wives were there en masse, but I was the most stuck-up one there...and the most frightened!

The following afternoon was my debut as teacher at Ming Deh. What a contrast! Some of the girls haven't had much English, so I'm to teach as much as possible in Chinese. They sing quite well. It looks promising. There are, so far, sixty girls, mostly seniors. Whenever my vocabulary flops, (every other word) I start clowning so they think I'm goofy I'm sure. It is easier to tell them about what is poor singing than what is good, so I have given all sorts of demonstrations from doughty opera would-be's to poor, timid, rabbit-like schoolgirls. I'll be teaching there two hours on Tuesday and Thursday afternoons and giving supplementary private lessons on Saturday afternoons.

I was also asked to lead the Nanking University Chorus on Wednesday nights. That is in English, so it should be fun. Did I tell you I was elected to the Board of Directors of the Nanking YWCA? In connection with that I serve as supervisor of the Home Women division: maternity clinics, nurseries, etc. This week seven members of the World YWCA are visiting Nanking, so I'll get in on a couple of nice Chinese feasts in their honor. One will be at the home of Madame Chang Chung whose husband is premier of China and one at the home of Mrs. Han Li-wu whose husband is vice-minister of Education.

Last Sunday night we entertained all four Presbyterian Chinese pastors, their wives, Bible women, plus all the Presbyterian missionaries in Nanking. It was to welcome some personnel who have just returned. A newly elected member of the Board in New York was also here. Ben was ill, so I found myself in the terrifying position at the beginning of entertaining ten Chinese who spoke no English. Whew!

Our money continues to be a disaster. This month we will pay our cook $550,000 Cn. When I first arrived we were paying him

$100,000 Cn. We hear that prices in America are spiraling, too. $1.15 for a pound of butter is bad.

Right now the queerest sounds are coming in the window from the street. A herd of pigs is being urged along by the farmer who is singing and cracking a long whip over their heads. Behind them are two button sellers who trot along crying their wares while keeping up an intricate rhythm on tiny drums. A rickshaw puller just tripped, lost his footing, and flipped his woman passenger onto her back with her feet in the air. She is screaming, he is swearing, and the policeman out there is merely looking on, doing nothing. And so it goes!

PEGGY KORDICK

Nanking, China
Monday, October 6, 1947

Last week was a whirl, but not too bad. The whole family was well, and that makes living easier. Monday the delegates to the World YWCA Conference in Hangchow arrived in Nanking, and I helped to entertain them. After a reception at the Y in the afternoon we all went to Lotus Lake for a Sampan ride. From there we were taken to the home of Mrs. Han li wu for a Chinese supper. Mrs. Han's husband is vice minister of education, and both of them are Han Chung Church members. The nine delegates were from Germany, Belgium, Canada, Holland, France, Denmark, and Indonesia. I particularly enjoyed those from Denmark and Holland. After the supper Mrs. Han asked me to sing some of the River Boat songs, so I did unaccompanied.

With missionaries returning to occupy Elmian House across the street, a large part of the furniture we have been using had to be returned to them. Much time this week has been wasted in shifting our things about, dumping clothes out of chests and drawers, and finding other places to store them. A most irksome task!

Dining table, ten chairs, three bureaus, eight small tables, two beds, buffet, two floor lamps, dressing-table and large mirror, and many smaller items: all went at once. Next month more people are expected to return. Then we will be left with nothing. The famous green trunks which brought my freight are back in service as much-needed storage space.

Friday night we had the Ch'en yu hua's over for dinner and a long conversation. Mrs. Ch'en is principal of Ming Deh and holds other important positions in Nanking. Her husband, a banker, is, among other things, the only elder under seventy years of age at Han Chung Church. Miss Mary Ch'en, his sister, is the spark plug of the church, teaches English at Nanking University, and serves on dozens of committees in the city.

All three of them are powerful in several different ways. Their power in Han Chung is a force we missionaries must understand and reckon with. They are eager to see a great future for the church, but they understand little about the methods of achieving it legitimately.

In China it is possible for a powerful few to wangle their own way in an incredible fashion. They are sincere in many ways, but their family's power in the city and in the government is so great that we wonder about their motives in church and school alike.

We had made plans to go to Hwai Yuan this weekend for a retreat. We thought we would go on Thursday and return on Monday, friends having offered to stay here and look after the children. Yesterday we were warned, however, that the Communists have surrounded Nansuchow and are in and around Pengpu. The latter place is the railroad terminal from which we were to have taken a boat on to Hwai Yuan. The former is just a few miles from it. Consequently, it looks like the whole thing will be cancelled. It's a good thing they decided to take it this week, for if they had waited until next week, we might have been stuck there for quite a while. In fact, the Hwai Yuan women and children may have to come here instead if matters get any worse up there.

This is a strange place. Except for the soldiers in uniform who crowd the streets, buses, etc., there is little evidence that there is a war anywhere around. But there is, and its influence hangs over us all the time.

We have had a rough time lately with our servants. If you are tempted to be jealous of us for having them, just put that idea right out of your thoughts. Now it is health problems. It is always something. From their physical exams we discovered that the old amah and her nephew both have triple trachoma, the cook and his family all have double trachoma, and the coolie has some kind of malaria. Besides this, all have roundworms and various minor and major infections of ear, nose, etc. and are anemic. The amah is suspected of TB as well (an X-ray this week will tell). The cook is a carrier of SYPHILIS! In America there would be no question of what to do. You would just fire them. But here—well, it's not that simple. Instead, tonight I start putting drops of zinc sulphate in their eyes, then send them once weekly to the hospital to have the lids swabbed. There's no use to tell you what else is involved, but it is certainly a mess!

The point is that everyone else in China has the same diseases, so there is no point to firing them and hiring others.

A cold fall rain has been drizzling down all day. I have a mean cold and Tom has impetigo, so I have spent the day at home with both kids in Tom's room—just playing. We have to be gone so much of the time that I get a gnawing feeling that the kids are growing up while I miss out on the major part of their lives. Amahs may sound like luxury, but I would a million times rather watch my own children. All our amah does is to carry Judy around and scold Tom—or ignore him. Judy is not the kind to enjoy being carried, so she snarls until put down and then snarls more because the amah keeps one hand on her shoulder and follows her around like her shadow.

The amount of time the amah cares for them shows up in direct ratio to their behavior. They are crabby and nasty if she's had them all day, mostly from sheer boredom. Both of them get a whale of a bang out of going for long bike rides with us, so we use that as our chief method of recreation. Ben takes Tom and I Judy and we peddle off. We usually head for the country, as the city wall is a short distance from our house. The crowds and dirt and dust in the city make city trips unpleasant. Judy draws an especially big response from the Chinese. They are quite shocked at our putting her on a bike; more shocked when they discover she likes it!

LIFE AND DEATH IN NANKING

Nanking, China
October 28, 1947

As I've told you before, I have had a difficult time liking China. The introduction I had was pretty rugged. How can I describe what it is like here? We bemoan crime in America, but compared to the vicious graft and organized vice that is part of everyday life in China, America's is small potatoes. They do not seem as barbaric as we. They do not have murders on so large a scale, but they have so many more sophisticated refined types of evil that it makes your head spin.

Care for the other fellow is not known, except among Christians, or so it appears to us. In traffic it is literally every man for himself. The consequent scramble and confusion is simply unimaginable to anyone who hasn't seen (or worse, almost been killed by) it.

Last week I gave a demo lecture at the Y on home arts and crafts. I had clipped pictures from American magazines to give them ideas on color combinations. Even though these were middle-income women, the idea of anything so grand as a small American bungalow with its bright curtains, tiled bathroom and spotless kitchen made them look at me with a "What do you think we are?" look, until I assured them that it was only the colors I was trying to demonstrate, not the rooms or furniture. I gave them ideas for making place-mats (but they eat from bare tables as a rule), curtains from the traditional women's underwear cloth of red plaid cotton, rugs and other little things we use to brighten up our homes. Most of it fell, I fear, on deaf ears. The basic idea, that of doing these things for oneself, is foreign to Chinese women. If they are wealthy they buy satin and velvet draperies and Peking rugs, porcelains of ancient and delicate beauty. With these they decorate their homes.

Otherwise, their houses range all the way from cheerless barns to pigpen-like crowded dens. Strong talk? True, though. This country is so full of tradition it is bound and trussed with it. For a Chinese woman to think of making her own curtains, even when she cannot afford tailored ones and her home is barren without them, is unthinkable. When they hear that American women do their own housework, they are astounded, and often frankly scornful. Work is a disgrace for all but coolies and farmers, and they do an unbelievable amount of it.

Laziness and industry are both national traits, depending upon which class you are talking about. When we arrived, we talked of asking some student girl to come and share our home, in return for which we would ask her to take part-time responsibility for the children. But could we find one? No. Students also are disgraced by manual work of any kind. It is difficult to understand and appreciate customs and traditions which so differ from our own.

Nanking, China
November 6, 1947

The morning of the 31st we took the eight-o'clock train to Shanghai after making arrangements for leaving the children in good care here. It was a glorious trip. The weather was perfect from start to finish, and we did nothing but enjoy ourselves the whole time. Of course, a certain amount of business had to be thrown in to justify the trip, but it was great.

My opinion of Shanghai had altered greatly. In fact, the city itself has altered greatly since last year when I arrived. My introduction was certainly unfortunate. Compared with Nanking it is very like stepping into Chicago or some other sprawly Western city. Shops are filled with the same things as yours. Everyone seems to be sleek and well fed. Real butter, chocolate, fresh milk, furniture, toys: all these things are found there. It gave me a jolt to see things like that being taken for granted again.

We went to a movie, *Frenchman's Creek*, a terrible one, but in lovely Technicolor, toured the city by pedicab, visited people, did some shopping, and had ourselves a good time.

On Monday we wanted to go to Hangchow, but the fact that three students and two professors were murdered there last week by Chiang Kai Shek's government made the city unsafe for foreigners, so we went to Soochow instead. It is on the rail line between Nanking and Shanghai, and is known as the Venice of China because there are almost as many canals as streets.

Soochow is sleepy, old-fashioned, almost untouched by the influences of America, so is fascinating to visit. We poked around in the shops there and came out with a 1500-year- old incense burner and a superb yellow porcelain plate with a green dragon on it. Such things are hard to find in China today, especially in Nanking.

We stayed overnight with a Southern Presbyterian couple whose bikes we borrowed for a ride out into the country. We saw many pagodas, canals, narrow, twisty streets, and dignified old men coming blinking out of their dark shops to pass the time of day with their friends.

Farmers were breaking up the soil for fall planting, harvesting late rice and wheat crops, their husky blue-clad wives beside them. An interesting thing about the country around Soochow which we do not have in Nanking is the abundance of graves sticking up all around. There doesn't seem to be one plot of land without at least one big sodded hump rising suggestively from it. Some of these have what look like doghouses with Chinese winged roofs built on top of them. These, I hear, house the spirits!

Tuesday morning we headed back to Nanking, arriving here at two-fifteen. We caught a ride on the American Advisory Group truck which meets every train. Our arms were more than filled with packages.

Today I am in bed with a sinus infection (?) which had me burning with fever yesterday. It is a glorious day and both kids are outside enjoying it. That is one good thing about servants...you can be ill and go to bed, and your household goes on as usual!

By the way, about the packages you send out here: on declaration slips they don't want to know how much it cost you, retail price. All that is dutiable is the wholesale price, or one-third to one-half of the retail price. If you value things retail, they charge us on that basis. Candy and toys wrapped as gifts and so declared are now allowed.

There is so horribly much graft, cheating and dishonesty in general that they really have to be tough about their customs regulations. Anything American sells for one to twenty times its retail value in the States out here. There are so many people importing things for speculation that the government cracks down on even such small items as "parcels from home," which makes it hard for us, but is understandable.

So few know what is happening in China. What you hear in the news is about 90 per cent wrong. There are so many half-baked "authorities" on China who don't even know enough about the situation to know that by talking too much they are making an already impossible situation worse! Congressman Judd, for example. Did I hear him? I'll say I did, and it made me sick. He doesn't seem to know that things have been going on in China ever since he left during the last decade, and that the China of today is not the same one he left.

That's a mistake many people make. Lots of old-time missionaries and even business people came out here about the time I did, and had the noble idea that they would help China "win the peace" or some such nonsense. They have found a China that shocks and bewilders them, and many have thrown up their hands and gone home—much to the delight of the Chinese.

People who live in Nationalist areas, like us, know all about the Communists, but very little about the Kuomintang. And vice versa. Both sides distort all reports about the other until who knows what the truth really is? It's just like the differences between Russia and America. Both sides want power, neither trusts the other...and there you are. Suspicion breeds outright distortion of news reports, people's minds get set a certain way, and then hate and all the other accompanying unworthy emotions get a real start.

Congressman Walter Judd comes over here and blows off about the fact that America has blood on her hands because we broke the gentlemen's agreement at Yalta to keep Manchuria for Chiang's government. What Judd hasn't apparently paid any attention to, is the fact that Chiang's government and China are not necessarily synonymous.

How the Kuomintang can get by with the things it does while we keep pouring money in to support it is amazing. Everyone knows about the Communist atrocities. How many know about the fact that, day after day, one person after another is being murdered by Chiang's government in the interest of "security"? What does America think is the significance of the suppression last week of the party that many people had gone on record as saying was the only hope for China's future?

Leaders of that party were seized, many killed outright, the rest will gradually disappear. We know. We had friends among them. They knew this was coming, but they did not flinch. Then your Judds come over here and expand their chests and roll out the words, "your great leader, Generalissimo Chiang."

Then there are the gullible missionaries. By this I do not mean that all missionaries are gullible. But out here there are many who are in the habit of thinking a certain way. They were told long ago that Chiang was a Christian. Magic word. From then on they shut their eyes to his policies and backed him per se. This kind of people

I have no use for. The world is in too much danger today to take time to listen to people who cannot see and think for themselves. And China's danger is more imminent and her tragedy greater. Because there are now only two sides, and both sides are very wrong, and no one is trying to help.

Last week a friend of ours who has twice been chased out of his North-China station, told us of the influx of Communists into heretofore-Nationalist territory. There are eight percent more of them in North China now than there were a year ago.

They are gradually winning this war. They do not hold cities. They capture, then run while the other forces come in to "defeat" them and then return to occupy a city after the others have gone elsewhere. Cowardly? Perhaps. But also wise—and lifesaving from their point of view.

The Lutherans are all pulling out from that area. They cannot work there once the Communists have taken over. Why? Because they are Christians? No. Because they are foreigners, especially Americans. The Communists have peppered their people with anti-American propaganda. As exaggerated as all propaganda always is. So when the Communists enter an area they look first for Americans and their satellites—often Christians. Why are they after Americans? That should be self-evident, but to refresh your mind, we have been supporting the Kuomintang with American money, equipment, men, and ideas for a good long time. And Americans here are made to seem the epitome of all the evils of capitalism.

Another good friend, a UNRRA fellow, came here last week after having spent six months in Cheefoo under the Communists, administering CLARA supplies when the Nationalists would let them through. He also told of the frank anti-American campaign being carried on, but said an attempt was being made to differentiate between American foreign policy and American people.

You can see how that affects us. If such an attempt were successful, we would not necessarily have to withdraw whenever the Communists came in. Unfortunately, however, such a differentiation is too subtle for the average victim of propaganda, and the peasant begins to think if Americans are as bad as the campaign literature says they are, he will do the cause a favor by shooting a few. So, if the missionary stays he gets shot, and then he is of no use to anyone.

Also, the Chinese Christians have trouble when the Communists find evidence of too much American influence in a given area. One of our Presbyterian people recently went blindly into Communist territory feeling very martyr-like and thereby put the lives of hundreds of Chinese, who had been her associates, in peril.

The situation is complicated. The world is also complicated. It is hard to know what to do. The presence of the American Army here definitely is a handicap to us missionaries. They do not know that, and feel that they are helping. But they live differently: they have lots of money, they have cocktail parties, they get drunk, and for a joke, murder Chinese fishermen — and they are here to help in a war that is distasteful to all lovers of China. So, the picture the Chinese begin to have of us is tragically distorted.

I spend most of my lesson time describing our home in America, family, and interests to these students to try to rectify some of their wrong impressions of us. But what good does that do? We ride our bikes, and Nationalist soldiers careening down the dusty streets in their American Jeeps swerve over, almost hitting us, grab our bike or our arm as we try to keep our balance and our temper, and leeringly shout: "Ding boo hao!" (This is the new version of the phrase called to American soldiers during and shortly after the war, "Ding hao," or very good. The present version expresses the current feeling towards foreigners more accurately — "Very bad").

One day I answered a knock on our door to find Dr. Chen, president of Nanking University, there. After we were seated and had tea and peanuts and Chinese cakes, he talked and I talked (about nothing of consequence). An hour and a half later (fast, by standards of Chinese etiquette) he began to tell me why he was there.

Since I am directing the Nanking University chorus and have sung for many public occasions in the city, would I put on a program for the student assembly featuring my singing of a variety of American college songs?

I was stunned. All I could think of was how absurd a young, blonde, American female would be attempting "Boola Boola"! In China we don't blurt out our feelings, especially when talking to University presidents, so I tried to discourage the idea rather gently.

Too gently. He thought I was just being polite, so he insisted. I was no match for him. To my absolute horror, when he left an hour later he had secured my promise to do it.

My accompanist and I started to work, but I dreaded the very thought. What happened? The day of the program a messenger arrived from the university telling me that because of the killing of a Chinese fisherman by some drunk United States Marines (or sailors) the students were all riled up and my presence on campus might set off a demonstration. My feelings of relief were boundless. I didn't think until later of the poor, dead fisherman!

And what of the Chinese Church? I can only speak for Nanking. Here there is very little that is encouraging. Very little. We were fed a lot of stuff about the Chinese having come through the war with their sense of Christianity refined and sharpened. In Nanking there is little evidence of this. Our most faithful attendant at our young people's group at Han Chung Church we discovered last week (with a terrible jolt) is the one who writes up the news of Nationalist Army "victories" for the papers. The fact that he is dealing exclusively in lies doesn't seem to have disturbed his "Christianity" in the slightest.

Ted Romig was questioning Pastor Pao (Han Chung) about our mission's country stations in this area. "There are no very good Christians," said the pastor. "What do you mean 'good Christians'?" asked Ted. "Oh, wealthy ones who can support the church," quickly answered the pastor. And that is a Chinese concept that it is well to bear in mind. The soul and body of a poor man are of no consequence. Those of a rich man are.

Are we discouraged? Of course we are. You can't be in alternate states of heartache and blood-boiling indignation all the time without being worn down to bitter depression by it. But we came out here because we believed Christ was the one answer to all this. And we still do. In fact, as these problems pile up on one another we are more and more convinced.

There were those who asked for technicians from America. They thought they could graft American progress ready—made on sleepy, now-corrupt old China. They were wrong, and they have found it out. China needs a change of heart, not machines. She needs a change of thought, not industry right now. Technicians do not supply these things. These come from understanding Christ and His way for human lives. So we'll keep working, even if they don't want us.

My teaching is going quite well. The Ming Deh classes are slower because I teach in Chinese and because the girls are younger and not so advanced in singing. They are responsive, so it is fun. My hardest job to date is to convince them that it is no disgrace to sing alto. When I tested their voices and assigned them to various parts, some of them looked like I'd insulted them. In Chinese music, the only female voice is a high, thin, piercing soprano, so that's all they admire. I took a recent *Time* magazine featuring Marian Anderson to show them that other countries admire contraltos.

The Nanking University chorus I'm directing this semester is pure fun. I use slow English. They were a bit suspicious of me at first, obviously thinking I was too young to do them any good. But the steadily increasing numbers have been encouraging.

PEGGY KORDICK

Nanking, China
December 14, 1947

Except for the stepped-up tempo of our activities, and Tommy's incessant questioning about "the Nitto Carist Chiuld" and "Sandy Claws," we would have few reminders that the Christmas season is upon us. There are no colored lights strung across the streets, no dazzling window displays. No loudspeakers blare out the beloved carols over the heads of shoppers hurrying home in the early darkness with knobby packages. Loud speakers there are. They caterwaul the very worst Chinese music...and always full blast! We do have daily processions of pilgrims, going from here to there and coming from there to here, in such numbers that their destination seems much less important than their utter misery in going and coming.

These do remind us of Christmas, for among them are many weary women riding on the backs of burros, many men stumbling along in the cold of December, leading their families on and on in their search for homes. But tonight...I'm homesick!

So homesick that instead of doing what I should be doing I've been sitting here looking at a picture of all of you. Oh, how good you look!! Sentimental? Tonight I'm incurable.

Remember the fun of going off to church Christmas Eve and trying to guess who was playing Santa? Then hurrying home to snatch a lion's share of the 19 year old Christmas wrapping so you could (behind locked doors) do wonders with the ten-cent gifts you'd bought that last afternoon? Then the jealousy over whether the oldest or the youngest should be first in the go-downstairs parade Christmas morning, and the impatience with Dad for being so slow starting the fire? And Dad's inevitable Christmas Eve expedition from which he mysteriously produced hard candy, nuts, and a big present for Mother.

Remember the lean Christmas, Mother, when the Ladies' Aide managed to shower you with blankets and whatnot which, when unwrapped, made a pile that reached above the arm of your chair? I remember so well going to your knee and looking as reproachfully as I could, reminding you that I had received only a Bible and a pencil! Then there was that tense, sad Christmas when Marge was thought to be dying in the hospital. The blue and silver ornaments we had put on the table stayed there days and days, looking cold and meaningless, and finally were put away without ever having caused any joy.

It is wonderful to have such a rich reservoir of experience to draw on when you're in a low mood, isn't it?

My Ming Deh chorus is to sing three nights in succession at a Christmas pageant at the school, again on Sunday morning and Christmas Eve. (My debut as a director.) The University Chorus I direct sings Sunday afternoon and evening, and I sing a solo that afternoon as well. So I'll be busy!

Ben is thrilled to have had published this week by the Christian Literature Society four pamphlets written in Chinese discussing problems of modern Chinese students and offering Christianity as the solution. He has had high praise from many educated Chinese, foreigners, and students as well. It will be useful to Christian workers all over China. This subject has not been dealt with before in print. I wish my Chinese were as fluent as his. He converses with ease. The only reason his lectures aren't equally easy is that he insists on such perfection in Chinese style that he agonizes over the preparation of long speeches.

Poor little Judy has been ailing for ten days now. We are worried about her. She has a fair amount of pep in the mornings, but every afternoon runs a high fever. Her right eye is badly swollen and red from a secondary infection. To see the little thing droop limply around here when we are so used to her pep and zip keeps us worried. We keep hoping she will feel better. Visits from and to doctors have not helped at all.

I'm expecting to be booted out of the mission soon. Last spring we were told to order diesel-burning stoves through the Shanghai office, since diesel is much cheaper to burn than coal here now. We did. We waited, and finally heard the stoves had arrived. When we were in Shanghai five weeks ago they had even cleared Customs. But we have not received them.

Meanwhile, it is bitterly cold. So I got mad and wrote the mission and demanded to know why Judy had to put her little hands inside my clothes to get them warm, Tom had to get a cold which left him deaf in both ears, I had to get acute sinus infections, and Ben his old horrible cough when if they had gotten moving our stove could have been here before the cold weather, and saved all this agony. I have since heard that "the stoves are on the way," but they still aren't here. We finally in desperation installed the hard-coal-burning Vecto which we had last year and borrowed coal for it. Hard coal is now $140 per ton here, so we might as well burn the gold!

Our foreign clothes are not as well suited to this weather as Chinese padded ones are, but those make you feel so stiff and stuffed that I'd almost as soon be cold. Picture me writing this letter. We won't count the layers of underwear, then a wool-flannel robe, a heavy sweater, and on my feet fur lined flight-boots outside of my regular shoes!

Judy seems better tonight, but the Dr. wants her in the hospital a few days to get this out of her system. She and the amah go tomorrow morning. She'll get good care there. The amah stays right with her...even sleeps there because the hospital has no baby beds, and babies might fall out of bed.

LIFE AND DEATH IN NANKING

Nanking, China
January 5, 1948

We brought Judy home from Ku Lou Hospital on the Saturday before Christmas, not altogether herself, but at least free from fever and ear infection for a while. Sunday night my university chorus sang like angels and made me very proud. Tuesday night we were actually at home, doing nothing.

Wednesday night was the payoff. There was a service at Han Chung which attracted at least three thousand people. Beggars, street people, I've never seen such a crowd. They all pushed, crowded, talked, even shouted. The confusion was indescribable! I could not hear the chorus I was directing, and I was standing directly in front of them.

As soon as I could, I escaped through the sparkling moonlit night back to our compound and "peace on earth." Ben and I then tried to wrap gifts, but were suddenly aware of a horrible noise coming from upstairs. It was little Judy gasping for air. Those first moments were pure terror. What do you do when your child can't breathe, there is no electricity and the house is stoney cold? When we woke her up she proved to be so cheerful that I calmed down somewhat, though her breathing was still very rough and noisy.

We decided it was croup and not pneumonia. We took her down to the kitchen where we heated water on the old stove for steam. In our haste the only thing we could find for a tent was a dirty tablecloth. When a group of carolers from Ming Deh came into the compound with lighted candles around eleven thirty we were all still in the kitchen by the stove, huddled under the tablecloth like a three-headed ghost. Carolers here start out around midnight and carol all night. We are expected to furnish food and drink to them no matter what unearthly hour they choose to arrive. Ben went outside to pass around the cookies, peanuts, and candy we had prepared for them, while I just waved from the kitchen window. We were still up steaming Judy at two when the young people from Han Chung arrived, so Ben went out again to pass food around and again I waved from the window. We didn't dare leave Judy alone, so Ben, bless him, dragged in a small mattress and some blankets and slept on the floor next to her bed for what remained of the night. Christmas Eve!

About six-thirty I awoke with the strangely close-sounding strains of "O Little Town of Bethlehem" (in Chinese, of course) prodding me into wakefulness. I groaned and turned over, then sat up in bed and looked cautiously out the window from behind the curtains. There on the front steps on his knees was an old Chinese beggar singing at the top of his lungs. I surmised at once who he was: an old "hu lee hu too" (moron) who has lived for a long time by pestering soft-hearted missionaries. When Ben went down he found the man praying fervently that we would be as generous as God intended that we should!

January 7, 1948

Now it is Wednesday morning, and this hasn't been finished. We've had some real excitement to tell you of. Monday night after we had been asleep for a few hours we were suddenly awakened by the most terror-stricken voice imaginable. It was our coolie, who had heard glass breaking, gotten up to investigate, and surprised a thief in the act of stealing books from our student center. The coolie gave chase. What we were hearing was his horribly cracked voice shrieking: "Kao Hsien Sheng, Kao Hsien Sheng" (Mr. Cowles, Mr. Cowles) on and on and on. He was mortally afraid, yet kept chasing the thief back and forth across our yard, through the bamboos and over the hedges without stopping that awful hoarse cry for help.

Ben jumped into his slippers and coat and was down the front stairs and outside in three seconds flat. In his haste, his slippers came off, so he dashed across the frozen ground barefoot. After a brief chase he made a flying tackle which landed the thief on his back. The coolie came trotting up, out of breath, still screaming "Kao Hsien Sheng," and with another reflex brought a baseball bat down on the thief's head. If Ben hadn't been there, the poor thief would undoubtedly have been beaten to a pulp (that is the Chinese way of dealing with thieves), but Ben merely tied his hands and legs firmly together with rope, locked him in the tool shed, and went for the police.

Now here's the funny part! Eleven policemen came back with him to get the poor, shivering little thief, a young fellow. The police officers had pistols and the others all had drawn bayonets! Honestly, it was like a comic opera. They had heard me screaming out the window (I was shouting directions from my grandstand seat in the second-story bedroom), and had gathered to see what the trouble might be. We are awaiting results. They took thief, bag of books, and Ben's rope to the station, and we went back to bed.

This morning three Nanking Seminary students came over. They shook their heads over our failure to tie the thief to a tree and beat him senseless. Christian Seminary Students!

Thieves have visited us several times recently, so maybe the police will this time get our stuff back. There were at least three others here that night, outside the wall giving the unfortunate fellow who was caught directions. They all escaped, and the fellow refused to tell on them, at least while he was here.

One night last week, we went for a walk about dusk. In a lonely spot on top of a hill, we found a woman crying and moaning and rocking back and forth on the ground in what seemed to be a terrible grief. After passing her and discussing whether we should try to help, we decided to turn back and try to find out what was the matter. At first she paid no attention to our offers to help, but finally she turned around and told us her troubles. This will be difficult for anyone to understand who knows how much time we have been spending on learning Chinese, but we didn't understand enough of what she said to even know how to start to help her! She spoke the same dialect as our amah, and I've told you how awful that is.

We persuaded her to accompany us back to Pastor Pao's house, but there she balked and would go no further. The most we accomplished was to demonstrate a friendly, sympathetic, and listening attitude, which we hope may have touched her heart in some way. It is so hard to understand and know how to be of help. They are so different from us. Their thoughts do not seem to resemble ours at all.

A group of six people is coming for lunch today to discuss what to do about the awful refugee problem in Nanking. Hundreds of thousands of them have been streaming into the city in past weeks. So far, almost nothing has been done to ease their suffering. They have come because of crop failures this year, partly due to the flooding of the Yangtze one more time. The government's inefficiency is appalling. They collect money, then do not even use what has been given! Our group is from the Union Church and is trying to find out how the foreign population can be of help.

Nanking, China
January 24, 1948

Two letters came from you yesterday, Mother, bringing cheer on a very cold day in the midst of the year's only blizzard. We seldom get snow here; the climate is very like Washington, D.C., but this year's supply came yesterday. The children and I went out to revive our Iowa Fox and Geese game in the unbroken expanse of our front yard.

Judy was a funny little figure in the cunning red snowsuit Dorothy sent her. It almost, but not quite, fastened over the brown coat and leggings which you sent. She was literally as broad as she was long, and when she fell, as she often did, she would just bounce and lie there like a little splash of crimson jelly, quivering with laughter. Tom and the dog enjoyed the game, but the dog, a recent acquisition of the "locking the stable after the horse is stolen" variety, would not stay on the paths, and Tom found it hard to keep from chasing her instead of playing according to rules.

You will be wondering what became of the thieves: nothing. The police are seemingly hand-in-glove with the pao-chang (block supervisor) and the thieves. Two nights after our thief was caught, someone broke into Han Chung Church and stole a big clock and four long wooden pews. How the police can claim they didn't see those going down the street is a mystery. The pastor's wife (Chinese) who is not to be trifled with, snooped around in carpenter shops 'til she found them, and, returning with a policeman, demanded their return.

More about the refugees. They are living in little huts made of rice-straw, smaller than the area of a double bed. We have gone out to view the situation, and worked hard to get the community interested in doing something to help them.

There is a group of Iowa farmers here acting as an agricultural mission, a very fine group of men. One of them came over one day saying that one of the Chinese dairies was pouring sixty gallons of whole fresh milk down the drain each day for lack of a market. We all but died. I didn't know there were any Chinese dairies in the first place, and to be wasting milk was one of the worst things I've heard, even in this country. Ben and this Mr. Johnson got the dairies to contribute their surplus to feed refugee children. Chinese do not like dairy products. Mr. Johnson's troubles in China would fill a book. Things perfectly obvious to an Iowa farmer just don't catch fire over here, and getting a new idea across is next to impossible.

Your letter showed quite a little concern over the turn events have taken here lately. They will be worse, according to all the reports we have. It is certain enough that the China Council has started to evacuate all personnel north of the Yangtze in the coming months; weeks perhaps, if advisable. Many of these people will be brought here. I'm beginning to understand the wisdom of the large mission houses. This may be a storm like others we have heretofore weathered, and not be as serious as many fear. It looks bad right now. We would be last to leave in any case, for until the government falls we should be as safe as we are now.

It will surely be a tragedy if, by the blundering of warmongers, we who are here with a message of love have to be sent home. This time the blow to Christianity in the Orient would be a serious one. There has not been time to help to adequately repair the ravages of war on personnel alone, and, while a nucleus will undoubtedly always be able to carry on, the strides that could have been made would be sacrificed.

January 26, 1948 (added)

The day this was started ushered in a terribly cold wave, the worst in most people's memories. For us it simply means we stay close to one or two rooms and that our water supply from the attic storage tank on down is frozen solid. The tank overflowed during last night, and some water dripped to the third floor and on down to the second floor. The bulk of it froze in the act of dripping, so we have the peculiar spectacle of icicles hanging inside the house from our third-floor ceiling.

Ben was summoned early this morning by a Chinese doctor from the big Central Hospital where conditions of suffering among refugees are indescribable. Many of them have frozen to death during the past few nights in their camp. Not a few have starved as well. I am ransacking the house this morning for any conceivable thing they can possibly use out there.

This afternoon we will go out to the camp with that doctor who has done more than anyone to help. We heard that the government has just issued an edict stating officially that there are no refugees, so no help will come from there. A good bit of clothing and a little food has been gathered by the foreign community, including many embassies, but a lot of help is needed in the gigantic task of distribution. The days of hard rains which preceded this cold snap were disastrous to those poor people, for their huts of rice-straw were washed away. Even those who did have padded clothes were so drenched that they have not been able to dry them out. You can imagine their condition when this extreme cold hit them.

PEGGY KORDICK

Nanking, China
February 2, 1948

We drove to the refugee camp in a big "Semi" ambulance today. There are thousands and thousands of people in raggedy tatters living (?) in raggedy straw shacks. I thought a lot of them had been coming into Nanking to beg because I had seen them on the streets the past weeks, but to see them huddled out in the "camp" en masse was staggering.

They began running toward us. We were quickly surrounded by a crush of struggling bodies. It seemed for a while as though they would tip the big ambulance over. Something had to be done—fast. I was elected to climb on the hood of the ambulance to talk and try to divert their interest at least briefly from the food they knew was in there.

It worked for a while. My blonde hair and the fact that I was speaking Chinese did it. I kept smiling and laughing and making crazy remarks. Then a little girl about eight or so was pushed forward by some of the adults. She said:

"Why do you have yellow eyes?"

I poked my eyes wider open and said:

"My eyes are blue. See?"

She said: "You are a foreigner, aren't you?"

I answered: "Yes. I am an American."

She looked triumphant. "We Chinese know all foreigners have yellow eyes. If you are foreign, you have yellow eyes."

Next she asked whether I had "shot that tiger."

"What tiger?"

"The tiger you are wearing."

Since it is so cold, I had put on an ancient fur coat from the "missionary barrel." She insisted with the same logic that it was well known that all foreigners were "tigers." That game was getting old, so she then threw me a real curve. Would I take her home? The adults around her told me she had no parents and no relatives at all. It took no great brilliance to foresee what would happen if I agreed to take her home. We would be mobbed and trampled.

Just then a Mennonite lady who had gone with us, took off after someone who had grabbed an armful of clothing from the back of the ambulance. She slipped in the mud, falling flat on her face. The crowd's interest was diverted, so I scrambled down, relieved to be out of the frying pan.

Even giving is hard out here!

PEGGY KORDICK

Nanking, China
March 30, 1948

You may have heard of the evacuation of women and children from Tsinan two weeks ago. All those people have been here, and we have enjoyed getting to know them.

I told you of our frantic Christmas. Want to hear about our crazy Easter? That morning was rainy, but by afternoon it had cleared off to a sparkling Spring day. What a day! The young people had planned a sunrise service on a nearby hill. When it rained, they came, unannounced, to have it here instead. They hid red eggs (or rather slips of paper "claim" as they feared the rain would wash the color off the eggs!) all over our yard, had their service, then hunted the eggs.

At nine-thirty I went to choir practice at Han Chung. Services began at ten. The choir sang four specials, plus amens and responses in Chinese. It lasted nearly three hours, what with baptisms, reception of members, music, and a play. I sang a duet in Chinese with a good tenor.

At two-thirty there was a Union Church service at Han Chung where our choir again sang the morning's numbers and our duet. Then I tore immediately out to where our cook had a rickshaw waiting to take me to the university to practice for a double quartet for the English service at four-thirty. We sang two numbers, in both of which I had long solos. That service lasted until six-thirty (because of Communion) when I jumped into the Army truck which dumped me at home by seven.

Ben and the children had eaten early, as Ben had to go to Han Chung to set up for our combined young peoples' service at seven-fifteen. After bolting my supper, I rushed over to help with that. When we finally sank down in our own dining room to eat hard-boiled egg sandwiches, dried apricots, cake, and cocoa, we were so exhausted we scarcely spoke a word.

Judy's mixture of Chinese and English would be tough for you to figure out. It seems to be much easier for children to learn Chinese than English, hence her Chinese words are greater in number and clarity.

Tom is getting tall, and, when he sheds his winter layers is slender as well. He's full of energy and ideas as usual, but is a lot of company. Guests comment on his hospitality and his self-possessed manner of making them feel at home. The other day he entertained an unexpected guest from Shanghai for nearly an hour while I finished teaching a class of girls in the Student Center.

If you could see how terribly often we are tense with worry over the success or failure of our work and discouraged over the mediocrity of it, you'd know that we cannot ever brag. As for the children, they are a wonderful blessing to us out here. They are brassy and naughty and absolutely impossible much of the time, but if we didn't have them to dote on we'd go absolutely berserk.

Tom and I have long conversations before he goes to sleep at night, and there's nothing quite so satisfying as to hear the evidences of his little mind at work. He is so sensitive to the enormity of the problems we face out here. I marvel at his understanding. His prayers are beautiful. He talks very naturally to God and tells him things to tell Jesus.

Last night he said: "Dear God, this was such a lovely day. Thank you for all the fun on our picnic and the lady who pushed our boat for us. Tell Jesus thank you for Easter, and we're so glad he isn't dead. Dear God, help all those people who don't understand about you and Jesus. Tell them that even when their friends die they don't have to be unhappy and carry those big, red boxes in the street. Tell Jesus to be with them to make them happy. Please tell Gramma and Grawmpa and Jawn we love them and we will come to see them some time in Newman, California, because they are there now and they wish they could see us. Amen." I don't think I've written all he said, but I haven't added or changed anything. He's quite a boy.

You sounded quite worried about us in your last two letters. Don't be. We won't be the last to leave if any real danger comes. If we are caught it will be because of something unavoidable. Things do look very black now, the worst they have since we came. Everyone says they think we'll either be sent home by summer or we'll be here another year at least.

The Tsinan people who were evacuated last week are beginning to go back up there, though, so you see even sometimes when danger comes, it passes shortly.

It's dark now and again no electricity. Guess I'd better get the kerosene lanterns started. No studying tonight.

p.s. Ben says the business about going home before summer is rot. Could be. Who knows?

Nanking, China
March 9, 1948

What a day! The sun was shining this morning, but even though it isn't now, the air is still warm and just loaded with Spring fever. The kids are outside with the amah I have spent all day boning up for my class at the university tomorrow. When they asked me to teach on music in film and radio it was about as preposterous as when they asked me to do a program of American college songs. But again there was no one else they could ask, so I found myself agreeing to try. There are few to no materials available, so I've had to devise a syllabus on my own using some books from my own college days, records from the United States Information Service, and library books from the same source.

They really worked me over at first. Their first test papers came back with absolutely identical answers. Aware of the dangers of causing any of them to "lose face," and equally aware of the deadly consequences of allowing myself to "lose face," I thought a lot about what to do. Finally, I decided to make a joke of it. I held up their papers and told them I had thought there were many students in the class, but had gotten test answers from only one. Or perhaps all Chinese scholars think the same thoughts at the same time? I let that sink in, then put their papers down and gave them a second test. That time the results were honest.

I manage to stay about one week ahead of them!

Yesterday we actually dropped everything and went on a picnic up on the city wall not far from our place, but far enough that the scenery is completely different, and crowds aren't likely to gather. I started ahead with Judy and our lunch in a rickshaw. It was a brilliantly sunshiny day, and the kids were just raring to go, for they've both been in a week with bad throats. My rickshaw man wasn't overly ambitious, and started off at a slow crawl, but Judy didn't mind. She waved and called and smiled at all the people on the street in her best stop-traffic manner. In China it does just that!

A pedicab trying to pass us hooked our wheel when the driver gawked at us at an extra awkward moment. A coolie tripped over a dog and splattered water from the wooden bucket he was carrying at the ends of his bamboo poles. A jeep-full of soldiers nearly collided with a huge six-by truck likewise loaded, when both drivers craned their necks at us. This, multiplied over and over, is what we experience any time we're on the street, particularly with either or both children.

Up a half-block from our house we turned left onto the big road which leads straight from the city gate to the heart of the city. It is only about a half-mile from there to the gate, and this we took at a leisurely amble. Along the right-hand side of the road, just past the corner, is the Nanking Theological Seminary grounds surrounded by a high gray stone wall. For a long block, the length of the wall, there is a solid row of mat sheds, populated by beggars living in a kind of squalor you have to see to believe.

The "walls" are either bundles of straw or woven reed mats about six by three feet joined together at the top by twine or string. The third wall is the stone seminary one. Fronts of these sheds are open. They resemble a pathetic, squalid version of little boys' blanket tepees. Large families live in these.

As we jogged along, we saw dozens of them sitting in the sun with blank faces, usually picking lice intently out of hair or garments which they had shed for the purpose. From my bedroom window now I can see a ragged beggar woman with two children (either hers or someone else's borrowed for the purpose) who have been running after pedestrians and rickshaws all afternoon. My windows are open, and I have been hearing, even at this distance, their high singing whine. Many of these are "professional" beggars. There are several of the women who on the coldest days will dress warmly themselves, but carry small children or babies who are naked and blue with cold to generate more sympathy.

To finish with the picnic: it wasn't long before Ben and Tom on Ben's bike had overtaken us, and we proceeded to the gate more or less together. There we turned to the right and followed along the foot of the immense wall for another little way. Finally we came to a place where there was a path to the top.

Dismissing the rickshaw, we then climbed up and walked along the top (20 to 30 feet wide) until we found a spot private enough for our needs, and we sat down, washed our hands in alcohol, opened our lunch and ate. Tom met disgrace by kicking over our thermos and breaking it, leaving us with only sandwiches, crackers, boiled egg and fruit — no drink. Sandwiches? Tinned meat spread and some apricot jam, both from UNRRA. Crackers? Gleaned from ancient (says 1943 on the label) Army boxed rations. Fruit? Bananas and tangerines—standbys since they have thick skins, so can be eaten fresh. We have them daily since we can have no fresh vegetables, fresh fruits of any kind are a necessity.

At other seasons we have had Chinese pears (not at all like our pears except in shape), persimmons and pummelos. We must drop all fresh fruit in boiling water for a few minutes. I even had the cook do this to the persimmons off our own tree, for we live so close to the street, and there is so much dust, and so many of China's diseases are dust-borne that I felt it wiser to be careful.

We came home after we had looked down on the other side of the wall to see the village squeezing smack against it. It wasn't long before knots of people were gazing up the vertical distance to watch us above them.

An hour after we'd returned, a fiery infection developed in my big toe. When the Dr. came he couldn't tell what it was, but ordered me to stay off my feet today. So here I am. It doesn't hurt much today, and I'll teach again tomorrow. You'd have laughed to see the amah and the cook's wife trying to convince me they knew more about what ailed me than the doctor did. The cook's wife decided it was an ingrown nail, and I just about had to beat her to keep her from hacking away at it. Then, when the doctor came, she hovered in the background, confessing afterwards that she then decided it must be something else, for which she also had a sure-cure.

She was so insistent on its virtues that finally, in self defense and in order not to hurt her feelings, I had to give her $20,000 Cn which she sent with her son to some place around here where they sell drugs. When she appeared with the stuff (sticky black paste, a white rag, and a piece of string to tie it on with), I lost my nerve and gently but firmly told her I would have Ben put it on for me later. She wasn't satisfied until she had found a black sock for me to put on to hold it all together. I did not use it. This morning I had to get up early enough to hide it securely before she came in. Before she could ask me about it, I said it was really wonderful stuff and thanked her profusely for getting it—thereby closing the subject. She was in here a few minutes ago asking whether I didn't want her to put on a fresh application! Oh, me! Life is complicated. Well, so much for local color.

Nanking, China
May 9, 1948

For various reasons the benefit concert I had planned to give this spring had to be abandoned. The piano instructor at Ginling College who was accompanying me felt it would be a shame to let all that practicing go to waste, so between us we cooked up a garden party tea where I would sing an abbreviated edition of the long program. Rather than to tell you about the other things that have happened this week and last I'll describe in detail what this involved.

To begin with, our place seemed to be the only one suitable for such an occasion. Last week we had several glorious spring days; some of them giving more than a hint of the summer's extreme heat which will come so soon! I alternated between being glad for the good weather and wishing it would hurry up and rain and get it over with before Saturday. I've watched the roses anxiously for fear they either would bloom too fast and be gone, or be too slow and not come out in time. Our coolie had home troubles, so two weeks ago we had given him permission to go off to his native province to straighten them out, provided he was back at a certain time. That time came and passed, and he had not returned.

The house was badly in need of scrubbed woodwork, refinished floors, washed curtains, window washings, etc. The yard had not been mowed this spring, so weeds and straggly bushes made it look pretty dreary. Our schedules are already too full, so there was nothing to do but hire outside workers to come in and help get the place scrubbed. The student center has had such hard wear that it has needed refinished floors, painting, plus the piano had never been painted after we had had a carpenter repair it when we first acquired it. ALL these things were done these past two weeks!

Three times the men who were refinishing the student center's floor had to do it over, because they didn't listen to our instructions, and did it all wrong. First they poured gasoline or something over it to clean it. The tar base in which the small boards were set dissolved and those boards just stuck straight up out of the floor like kindling.

That fixed, they proceeded to paint the floor a ghastly sickening color of yellow-orange dear to Chinese hearts, but impossible from our point of view. All we wanted was clear varnish and wax, but when they finally finished at two-thirty yesterday (the guests were due at three!) what was on there was a mess impossible to describe: sort of buff-colored, nary a grain of wood to be seen. Those men do not appreciate the beauty of wood itself. Their idea is to cover it with all sorts of fillers and lacquers until a hard, shiny finish is obtained. With that we will have to be satisfied, I guess, because there wasn't time to ask for any changes.

Plans were made for what to do in case of rain, but all the time I had the idea that it wouldn't.

To make a long story shorter: Thursday was a beautiful day. I thought, oh, dear, if this were only IT. Because with the double-doors taken out and heavy furniture reduced to a minimum our place is still hardly large enough to accommodate 100 people comfortably. When we came outside from attending a station supper on Thursday evening, I smelled rain. Ben says that's a gift reserved for Iowans, for he can't. But I was sure of it. The wind blew hard all night, and when Tom and I were returning from Ginling (where I'd gone for my last practice with the accompanist) Friday morning the rain began.

Such a rain I have never seen. It was like Niagara Falls. In no time at all our whole front lawn, so carefully mowed and rolled, was flooded. I recalled hearing that it had been that way before I came, but since I've lived here it hasn't rained that hard. It kept coming and coming until the streets were rivers. Rickshaw men refused to take passengers except for outlandish fares; the lightning and thunder added their bit to the general excitement. It was really a storm.

Ben had asked a girl from the Seminary over for lunch. She arrived in the middle of the worst of it. The rickshaw man who brought her pulled her right into our compound and up to the front door, an unheard of thing to do. The rain was coming so hard we could scarcely see him leave our front gate.

That took care of plans for a garden party, so we began to work out how the crowd could be taken care of inside. The crazy coolies thought it all a big joke, and continued to trot across the lawn right through the water, carrying heavy boxes out of the student center and cleaning the lawn just as though the sun were shining. They looked like men from another planet in their odd assortment of Ben's raincoats, their big waterproof straw hats, and extra rubbers we found in our closet for them to put over their straw-sandal-shod sockless feet.

To complicate matters, on Thursday night late a fellow from Hwai Yuan and his seven-year-old daughter arrived without warning, expecting shelter. The little girl proved to have a fever and was obviously fighting a bad cold, so I overran their objections and clapped her into bed the next morning after giving her aspirin.

But do you know what? Saturday morning came with a cloudless blue sky, the sun grinning down as though he'd just played an enormous joke on us, and proceeded to dry everything up. By noon the only trace of the storm was the crystal clarity of the air and the sparkling greenness of grass and trees. Roses lifted their sodden heads and opened their petals to dry them out; the marigolds and pansies straightened up and looked brighter and prettier than ever. The lawn which the day before had been a huge lake just seemed to gratefully soak in the much-needed moisture and showed no ill-effects whatsoever. It wasn't even soggy, except in a few out-of-the-way and easily avoidable spots.

We couldn't believe it. Ben flew around assembling lawn chairs, hurrying the workmen, lending a hand here and a strong back there until by three o'clock there wasn't a more lovely spot in the whole city than our own place. We made a long table by placing a number of the gray tables from the student center end-to-end. On them I placed my best white tablecloth, a flat glass bowl holding an arrangement of pink and white roses, some new Chinese-made silver candle holders, plus my silver hurricane lamps–and the food.

Many exclaimed over the beauty of the "garden." The day and their pleasure at having such a party made it worth all the agony of preparation. By four-fifteen most of them had arrived, so we moved more chairs inside the student center and asked people to find places either outside where they could hear and see through the opened windows or come inside for the music. By the last group I was getting tired and tense, so had to change the last number to an easier one. All in all, it left us with a deep feeling of satisfaction. The guests (a mix of Embassy, Army, and Mission personnel) were very appreciative.

Well, that's a long tale, and maybe not a very exciting one at this distance, but it gives you an idea of what has occupied our extra (!) time lately anyway. Today has brought another downpour of steady rain. So you see, we had a miracle.

In three more weeks the operetta at Ming Deh will be presented. The work goes on. Ben has a conference during the first part of July, so he will take us to Kuling a little early and come directly back to work, then join us later. We may have to leave here as early as the first Tuesday in June. We still don't know. Transportation is still uncertain. We aren't sure whether to fly or go by boat again. Flying takes two hours, boat, two days! Tom thinks that next to America, Kuling is the best place on earth, so he is raring to be up there. The freedom up there does him lots of good. He prayed a strange prayer the other night: "Dear God, help all the people that you're blessing all the time."

Judy scolds Tom just as severely as he has scolded her at times, and reproves him soberly when she thinks he is not behaving properly. It's a riot to hear her try to sing "Holy, Holy, Holy" (which we use as a grace at the table quite often), If she is settled before we begin the prayer, she'll stretch out her hand to take ours and sing out "Ho-ee, Ho-ee, Hoooeee" in three different pitches—not the right ones, but Tom doesn't even hit those!

Last night friends asked us to go to an early movie and on to eat Chinese food as relaxation after the strain of the day. We were really too tired, but went and enjoyed the movie (Mildred Pierce) very much, and the restaurant, too. I marveled at the distance I'd come since last year, as the place was disgustingly dirty and crowded. We had to go through a garbage-heap and other unpleasant things to get in. Phew!

Nanking, China
Sunday, May 23, 1948

This is a darkish, quiet Sunday afternoon. Ben had a chance to fly to Peking with the Air Attache at the Embassy. The servants are greatly impressed over the fact that he left our gate at eight-thirty this morning and was probably in Peking by the time we ate lunch. Peking may fall any time the Communists decide to take it, so Ben was anxious to see it before that happens. Also, there are two promising divinity students at Yenching University he needed to interview for possible hiring as assistants in the youth program here. I'd like to have gone, too, but, aside from the children, have a massive rehearsal tomorrow afternoon at Ming Deh for the operetta which is to come off on Saturday the twenty-ninth.

Speaking of that, we had our first all present rehearsal yesterday afternoon from one-thirty until six. Pretty awful, but I have boundless faith in Chinese kids' ability to snap things into shape at the last minute. They don't know the meaning of planning ahead. They always seem to throw themselves into eleventh-hour frenzies, so I am banking on that. Plus rehearsals Monday, Tuesday, and Wednesday to pull them through. It will be a two-hour performance with songs, dances, and dialogue, so rough to do, but they are enjoying it thoroughly. Nothing like this has ever been tried in Nanking before.

The name of the operetta is *Ask The Professor*, one I was in high school. The Ming Deh principal has had the whole thing translated into Chinese, so that is how we're doing it. I could never have survived without her constant help. We mimeographed the songs and the leading characters memorized their parts from a single hand-copied master-sheet of the translation. American audiences would be astonished at how much has been done with so little equipment and time.

My classes at Ming Deh and the university both will wind up this week. Then begins the rush to get ready for Kuling. We still have no place rented there, but hope to have boat reservations for the week of June eighth.

The Chinese Government has finally granted Ben the money to start on a youth center project at Han Chung Church and a school for refugee children at Hsia Kuan. Now comes the pressure of seeing to it that the money ($15,000,000,000 CNC) is administered honestly: a superhuman job.

Nanking, China
June 8, 1948

This has been a killer of a day. The famous Nanking heat has arrived with a vengeance, and people are miserable after only a few days of it. It is like Washington, D.C's humidity. This afternoon I laid down for a short rest, then got up and took a sponge bath with cold water. Before the water had all been wiped off I was already streaming with perspiration. Poor Judy is so fat that she has been most uncomfortable. Prickly heat hasn't started yet on either of the kids, but I think it's only because I've given them whole or part baths three and more times a day. I say I, but don't mean exactly that.

We have hired a new amah who is working out much better than our old one. We had been very unhappy with that one. She had worked for the Mills for about twenty years, and had bound feet, so couldn't do things we need done on this immense place. Once I made up my mind to fire her, I was aware of how she'd been wearing me down.

I never felt I could quite trust the old lady, and she had absolutely no control over the children. One day, for example, we looked out into the yard and saw Tom chasing around with the cook's huge meat cleaver. The amah was standing there grinning foolishly at him, and making no effort to do anything about it. She also seemed to have something political going on, as there were almost nightly gatherings of men of all ages in her tiny room. One night I counted twenty of them as they left.

We have to pay more for this new gal, but she has a high school education and can read Chinese stories to the kids, sing songs to them, and she's taught primary school in the past, so she's a completely different type. I like her a lot, and hope she decides to stay here permanently. We had a difficult time persuading her to come. She was working for a young American couple who just left for home. Before she heard of us, she had tentatively agreed to go be some general's wife's sewing woman. She much prefers caring for children, however, so we were able (with the help of a Chinese "middle man") to persuade her to try us!

The operetta is over! We gave it last Friday and Saturday nights before about 6,000 people altogether, and it was a great success. The idea of extracurricular activities is rare in China, so we weren't given much time to practice. For a long time things went exasperatingly slowly, but finally, the last minute, they whipped it into shape. The hardest thing was getting the idea across in the first place, since nothing like it has ever been given here, and only in Shanghai has any ever been seen.

The girls were absolutely beautiful. They borrowed most of my wardrobe, past, present, and future, and all I could scrape together from friends. There was one scene where a Queen of May is crowned. Remember my white chiffon evening dress with gold beading? I haven't been able to wear it for four years, but brought it with me anyway. Believe me it met its destiny when it appeared on that Queen! I couldn't keep the tears out of my eyes as she came on stage. I have never seen anyone so absolutely beautiful and sweet looking. There were gasps of admiration all over the audience. She wore a crown of pale pink carnations. It was gorgeous.

We thought we were all through with the thing for this year, but the AAG got wind of it and asked us to put it on in their auditorium tomorrow night as a part of their cultural relations program. We took all seventy of the girls over there this afternoon for a rehearsal. It would have been fun to have heard the comments of the American high school kids who were standing around watching, if I hadn't been too busy calming my jittery girls' nerves at the strange surroundings and new accompanist. It is two hours long, so takes a long time to rehearse.

How I wish I could talk with you! We are so burdened with problems and have no one to discuss them with. The others in our mission are so much older that they don't help. They probably wouldn't mind having us confide in them but all they ever say is, "oh, you are so young. When you have been here twenty years as we have, my dear," etc., etc., until we just clam up and don't say anything. One man in particular has the most negative attitude I've ever seen. He is full of reasons why this and that cannot be done, and talks all the time about evacuation and how this and that place will soon be folding up, until it's terribly hard to go on thinking in constructive terms about anything, even though we are more or less certain this government will last another year or two.

Added June 10, 1948

Now the operetta is finally over. The day we performed for the AAG was horribly hot, the girls were faced with examinations and an athletic meet the same week, but they threw themselves wholeheartedly into it, and did even better than they had on their own stage. At one point a fuse blew, and the whole place was in darkness, but the girl who was at that moment singing a solo went on without a quaver. The chorus came in without direction, since they couldn't see me; another girl went on with her solo, and, though the accompanist was forced to drop out, since she couldn't see the music, the girls went on to the end of the number and finished it just as the lights came back on. I was very proud of them.

The last minute one of the girls in one of the dancing choruses was ill, so they commandeered a new girl, taught her the complicated routine of the gypsy dance they were to do during the first part of the performance, and when their turn came to perform, she did so perfectly that I did not know until afterwards that the substitution had been made! For Chinese kids a stage is a fairy carpet. They love it.

The only disappointment of the whole affair was the general attitude of our beloved countrymen, who made me utterly ashamed of my nationality. After big promises and a lot of blurby talk, they only managed to get about thirty people out, the rest were all children and high school kids and servants. The high schoolers I was glad for, of course. Then only two people came up afterwards to thank Mrs. Chen for the tremendous amount of effort she had poured into this extra performance, and those two did it in a condescending spirit that made me sick. She's so sweet, though, that when I talked it over with her the next morning she said, "Well, even if one person learned something and really enjoyed it in the way you and I meant for it to be enjoyed, it was worth it. Unpleasantness need not be remembered."

#129 B
Kuling, Kiangsu, China
June 18, 1948

As you can see by the heading, we're in Kuling again. Before we left we rented our Nanking house to some of the American Food and Agriculture people for the summer months. They will pay $120 gold per month, of which we get half and the mission gets half. They use two of our servants (the cook's wife and our coolie) and pay them. They jumped at the chance because, otherwise, they'd have spent the summer in the hotel they live in the rest of the year—hot and crowded. As they are mostly farm people, it means a lot to them to be in a place where there are grass, flowers, and a little feeling of roominess.

We had thought the boat wouldn't go until Monday (the last operetta affair was on Wednesday night), but on Thursday afternoon came a frantic note from the Longs (an Episcopalian couple who were also going) saying that it was leaving on Saturday morning. What a furor from then on. Notes flew back and forth, across the city, and all was more than confused.

The Chaffees from Hwai Yuan wanted to go with us, but were awaiting a telegram to tell them when. The wire was hastily sent. It ended up in the wrong province! By the grace of God they themselves decided it was time to come and arrived on Friday evening at our front door. Mary was quite harassed because she had left Cliff and most of their forty pieces of luggage mired in deep mud at the other end of the railroad line — PenPu. She and small Paul and tiny John William ate a bite at our house and then went to the Jones' for the night.

Saturday morning we got one report after another about delays in sailing. Finally, after a nice supper at the Moffatts, we got on board at ten PM in a drizzling rain which did practically nothing to dispel the oppressive heat.

Then came the exhausting task of getting our twenty pieces, the Winn's twenty-five, the Long's eighteen pieces of luggage on board, not to mention herding Tom, Judy, our cook, amah, and me, Nancy Long, her baby, amah and cook, the Winn's cook and his daughter. Finally, we were all on the dock, coolies had been paid, the servants had found places to spread their p'u k'ais (blanket rolls), and all seemed to be well.

We were traveling first class Chinese, as were the Chaffees. All the other foreigners on board were up higher in what is called "Salon" or special class. The Chaffees brought so much luggage because they may not be able to return to Hwai Yuan due to the Communists.

Our cabin was a tiny 8 foot by 10 foot affair with wooden slat bunks on two sides, a bench on the third. Outside our tiny window was the narrow deck on which every available inch was covered with people sleeping piled on top of each other, The smell of the air which those hundreds of closely-packed steaming bodies (not to mention our own) gave off was awful! No toilets were available, so mothers just let their children go on the floor. We discovered that our own and the Winn's servants were asleep sitting up on their piled-up luggage outside our cabin door, so Ben went out and moved some people around who were taking up more than their share of space, making it possible for our servants to stretch out at least.

Don't imagine that our cabin gave us any luxury. It was only a certain degree of refuge, that was all. The air was stifling, so we were forced to leave our door open, and all night long a man with TB who was at our doorsill kept coughing and coughing in long, exhausting spasms. It didn't help us to sleep, but I kept remembering that on the blanket next to his was a mother with two very small children.

The only food was Chinese, and very bad at that, so we kept the kids as much as possible to hot rice. I had brought a bunch of bananas and a few sandwiches and cookies along, thinking that we had only one day's meals to cover, but we reached one unloading station, Anking, at one a.m. of the second night, and because of martial law were unable to start unloading until six a.m., so we lost ten hours there.

We finally reached Kiu Kiang after nine on Monday night. The Methodist ladies who were so hospitable to us last year had a man at the wharf to meet us and escort us to hot baths, clean sheets, and a good night's sleep at last. I forgot to mention that the cabins on the boat were alive with bedbugs, lice, and roaches, and only a solid hour spent with concentrated DDT powder made it possible to sleep or even lie down.

Thursday morning we ate a leisurely breakfast. While the rest of us shopped a bit and prepared to go up the mountain after lunch, Ben went to see our baggage and servants sent ahead. The same battle with carrying coolies came off this year as last, We were delayed almost an hour and a half at the foot of the mountain while convincing them that we really could not afford to be gypped even if we were foreigners. We were finally grumblingly borne up. I was last, and my coolies were the meanest, so Judy and I arrived nearly an hour after the others.

We had rented a house from an agent, sight-unseen, and at first look were keenly disappointed in it. The floors were piled with dirt, and everything was in bad shape. Some Embassy friends had arrived at a nearby house the day before. They invited us to a delicious supper. When we returned, we made up our cots and crawled wearily into bed in the midst of the mess. By morning it looked a little more possible, however, and amah and I tore into the job of scrubbing everything with disinfectant and getting the place livable.

There is a large family of peasant "squatters" here in the servants' quarters. They obviously had occupied the house as well before our arrival. Under those conditions you don't feel safe until every inch has been disinfected. There is a large verandah which looks out across the mountain tops, making up for the fact that the house is dark inside, and repairs have not been made.

Our summer seems to be taken care of, but our fall plans involve some things we haven't told you before. We are expecting a baby about the fifteenth of September. I'll be up here until the latter part of August, then probably fly back, getting there just in time to do last minute arranging before the baby comes. I didn't tell you earlier because from this distance there are enough things for you to worry about, so why add another?

There is a good Chinese obstetrician in the Drum Tower Hospital who is handling my case, so you don't need to be concerned on that score. As I've been extra careful to avoid salt, the swelling I had last time hasn't even started.

The RH business they have no facilities for testing, so we'll all have to have faith that that, too, will be taken care of. I have been feeling fine. Even with the heavy schedule this spring I have done very well.

Judy's latest and most powerful phrase is, "Not yet." She finds that brings a laugh instead of a frown as a flat "No" does, so she makes the most of it. Our new amah is more of a companion to the children than our last one was, and we are very pleased with the indications of her influence even after two weeks. She speaks the Peking dialect (same as ours), which is a welcome relief after the unintelligible gibberish the Mills' old servant spoke.

Well, it is pitch-dark out here on the porch now, and the bugs are flocking around my kerosene lantern, so I think I'll go inside and crawl into bed to read a while where they can't get at me.

Kuling, China
Sunday, July 4, 1948
4:45 P.M.

The sun is shining brightly across the nearest mountains and into our veranda where Tom and Judy are playing. Somewhere a group of people is singing hymns, for I can hear them faintly now and then. Nearer sounds come from the stream which gushes noisily past our back door and the children playing in and beside it.

Hsing Hsin, our new amah, has gone off somewhere for a walk, while the cook is entertaining several old cronies in his room back of the house. Tom and I are taking it very easily because we ate some bad food which poisoned us on Friday night, and haven't been good for much ever since.

Ben wrote that he had made a trip to Shanghai to see whether the reconstruction money granted him couldn't be put into US gold, so saved intact until fall. Chinese currency has deteriorated so fast that what was a request for $30,000 US in March is now $250 US. Isn't that awful? Getting it put into US currency makes it possible to wait until fall to proceed with the building program it is intended for.

CNC has gone wild this month, but our salary, supposedly based on expenses, is the same as last month's for some unknown and better-be-explained reason. We don't know how we'll make it through the month. Ben and I have some gold which we can cash to get us through, but others aren't as lucky.

Kuling, China
July 7, 1948

The box you sent may have gone through some things while still in your hands, but that was nothing compared to its adventures since then! Ben made three trips to the post office in Nanking before he found them open and ready to release it to him. Then he took it home and put it in a heavy duffle bag along with Tom's rain coat and my boots and other odds and ends we'd left behind. Then he toted it over to the Moffatt's where it was put on a truck and taken to the rice-boat with their Kuling-bound luggage. They were on board ship two days and nights. When they arrived in Kiukiang early Thursday morning, they found that coolies were on strike.

So, after it was unloaded from the rice-boat, the duffle stayed at the "go-down" (warehouse) of a bunch of skinflints known as CHINA TRAVEL SERVICE. The Moffatts came up here by chair after a two-hour delay spent haggling with unruly coolies. The stuff stayed in Kiukiang. Friday morning I went to their place to help; I found them in a horrible mess.

Coolies were yelling at their doorstep, women were hanging around waiting to be employed as toilet-dumpers or grass-cutters. As the Moffatts speak no Chinese, I pitched in and tried to settle a few of the arguments. I soon found myself in the middle of a swarm of screaming, gesturing people, so retreated behind their porch doors to reconnoiter. Their baggage began arriving, and the din increased.

I then asked the Moffatts to eat lunch at our place. We eventually escaped, leaving their cook in charge of the free-for-all. Just as we reached a narrow, wooden bridge over a waterfall on our way home, another batch of coolies met us, carrying more of Moffatt's stuff, and there was my duffle! Our name in large letters was on it. They went on to Moffatt's and we in the opposite direction, but I had asked Dr. M. to bring it over if it arrived before he came for lunch. Two hours later he managed to free himself from the mess and started for our house and lunch. Half way here he remembered the duffle and trotted back after it. His respect for the coolies increased after toting the thing over here. One of them had toted it clear up the mountain!

At last they finished lunch. I could scarcely spare the time to see them to the door before rushing into the bedroom to unpack the duffle. It was a good fifteen minutes more before I managed to pull and heave the box out, it had been wedged in, quite obviously, by a man.

Judy, bright-eyed, perched on the edge of her cot and shouted "Pitty, pitty!" "Ziss is mine?" or "Ziss Bobby's" (she calls Tom Bobby) as I took the things out. The things are all so wonderful! I just cannot tell you how much I appreciate them, because telling simply isn't adequate!

#64 A Kuling, Kiangsi
August 3, 1948

Your letters come through up here almost as fast as they do to Nanking. This in spite of the recent airplane strike and consequent cutting off of the plane direct to Kiukiang. Can't remember when I last wrote. It must have been at least two weeks ago. Our life here hasn't been particularly smooth.

Judy was discovered to have a bad case of (round) worms. Tom fell down on our cement verandah and cracked the back of his head open that same day. I was beside myself. Completely lost my head. If it had not been for the intelligence of our amah, Tom would have been much worse off than he was. His mother was certainly a flop.

Something about the "splat" his head made when it connected with the sharp stone, combined with the horrible gush and spurt of blood which followed, just paralyzed me. I picked him up and rushed into the house, crying harder than he was, but I couldn't think what to do. The amah started putting cold wet cloths on, and before the doctor got here the bleeding had all but stopped. I did have sense enough to scream at the cook to run for Dr. Trimmer who lives above us. He dressed it with Sulfa powder and bandages, and it didn't turn out to be at all serious. It certainly could have been, and was enough to scare me silly.

Because of the air strike I hadn't received word that Ben was arriving. I was in bed reading, therefore, when his heavy tread came through the house to my door. He looked awful. He was positively all eyes. He had lost something like twenty pounds in the four weeks since I'd seen him. His terrible thinness combined with the fact that he was literally streaming with perspiration, and so exhausted that he could scarcely speak, made him look like some lost refugee. The boat trip had been nightmarish. The boat was so jammed with people that at least one person was trampled to death in the rush of boarding.

When they got to Kiukiang the city was flooded, so they had to come to the foot of the mountain by sampan. Then there was the inevitable sickening fight with carrying coolies before they finally started up the mountain about nine p.m. He hadn't eaten, so our cook and I fixed a hasty supper, got him a bath, and then let him go to bed.

There are many people who have come here this summer sort of between stations, having been run out of their permanent ones by Communists. In Nanking, while we have antiforeign demonstrations and riots, we simply haven't the awareness of the real war situation. Many of these people have been captured and held by the Communists.

We are doing our best to become acquainted and have talks with as many as possible so that our own picture of what is happening and what may be about to happen is more complete. Almost without exception these people have lost everything they had except the clothes on their backs and perhaps a few things they might have had sent out to some unbesieged point before the attack came. In every case it is plain that it is Americans the Communists are after with their worst venom. Chinese who have too intimately associated with Westerners are subjected to like treatment. They beg us to get out before the attack comes so they won't be forced to pay for having been our friends.

One couple, who we knew in language school, are here along with the man's father, who was one of the last to leave the Kaifeng area. The story of his and another elderly man's escape by donkey cart at the last minute is hair raising. Kaifeng is one of the places the Communists have taken and destroyed this summer. The Southern Baptists lost heavily in property there. The city was leveled.

Here in Kuling it is hard to realize that there is a war anywhere. The military police who plagued us so last summer aren't even here this year. More and more it looks as though this next year may be our last in China, however. No one really knows.

Last night there was a concert in a local auditorium similar to civic buildings back home. We had a concert last year, but this was more ambitious and better attended. Among others it included a Swiss organist, a French pianist, a British reader and some American singers in addition to me. I sang three Negro spirituals. One, "Sometimes I Feel Like A Motherless Child," must have caused some chuckles, considering that I am obviously pregnant!

Before I finish this I want to answer your question about Drum Tower Hospital. It is the University of Nanking Hospital, in the running of which our mission cooperates with six others. Dr. Daniels

Daring student riots

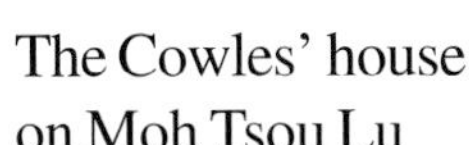

The Cowles' house on Moh Tsou Lu

Street accident

The servants (lower left) watching a parade in front of the Cowles' house

Han Chung church adjacent to the Cowles' home in Nanking

Interior of Han Chung church

Children selling bread on Moh Tsou Lu

Peggy in refugee camp, Nanking-1948

Refugees

Refugees

Refugees

Burial of baby Ben in the Foreign Cemetery, Nanking. Standing l. to r. Tsi Ping I, Gardner Wini, Ted Romig, Andy Roy, and Ben Cowles.

Peggy's first outing after the death of baby Ben

Operetta performed by girls of Ming Deh Girls' School and conducted by the author in Nanking, China

of our mission is the Superintendent. Dr. Trimmer and Dr. Moffatt are the only other foreign personnel at present, excepting a Jewish refugee doctor who has only foreign patients, I believe.

The hospital is adjacent to the university, though not on the campus. Martha Jones says the doctor is very good, and the food and nursing care are excellent. She says the staff is always excited about the arrival of a foreign baby, and knock themselves out to be of help. So, don't worry. We'll be all right.

Kuling, China
August 16, 1948

You would have been fascinated had you been present at the Community Church service here last Sunday. The Generalissimo and Madame Chiang had arrived in Kuling with a large entourage early in the week. We were nearly late for church, but came puffing (I, at least) down the hill just in time to meet them at the foot of the steps. Naturally they entered first. The only seat left for us right behind them. I'd have thought there would have been security men there, but there weren't.

Tom kept buzzing something in my ear. I finally heard him. "Mother, why doesn't the gen'issimo have on his reins and his guns?" Soldiers are Tom's ruling passion right now and most of them have crossed leather straps ("reins!") holding their guns. Hence his question.

This has been a wonderfully refreshing summer. An American Army Sergeant died of heat exhaustion in Nanking a few days ago, so you know the Yangtze Valley heat we write about is real. We feel very lucky to be away from it.

Plans are underway for our return, however. Harry Allen, a missionary's son who is now in the embassy as Naval Attache, has arranged for us to fly back the morning of the thirtieth in the U.S. Naval Attache plane along with his own household. Mary Lu, his wife, is expecting a baby just two weeks later than mine, so they're sending the Navy doctor up to escort our party back—just in case!

Tom is ecstatic over the idea of at last (his words) having a chance to fly. We think our baggage will be able to go along, too, so that will certainly save expense and trouble for us. The servants will go back by boat. We will have to spend one day at the Winn's house as the people who have rented our house for July and August will not leave until the evening of the thirty-first.

Living expenses have done some dizzy jumping this summer. Actual costs in gold are not really high. The rub comes because we are paid in CN and it is impossible to estimate the rapidity with which the exchange will alter, so we inevitably get caught without enough money and have no way of getting any.

For example: when we came here in June I gave the cook about $400,000 CN per day for food shopping. The past week I had to give him two silver dollars (Chinese), or approximately $12,000,000 CN. In terms of gold at the black market exchange rate, this is only about $1.10, but we have no gold.

You asked how the children spend their days. Hsing Hsin, our new amah, usually appears around seven a.m. to bathe and dress them. After breakfast Tom often scoots off to some friend's house. I straighten things up, give the cook his day's orders after taking accounts on how the previous day's dollars were spent) and keep Judy occupied until Hsing Hsin has finished overseeing the mopping of floors, making of beds, sorting of dirty clothes, etc., which the squatter Chinese woman who lives here does. Then Hsing Hsin takes Judy off somewhere for a walk, and I attempt to settle down to a morning of writing. In addition to keeping up correspondence with friends, we have to keep sending accounts of our activities to six different supporting churches back home.

If it is a nice day we take the kids up to the Methodist swimming pool for a swim before lunch. Since last year more work has been done on the bamboo pipes, so the water is cleaner and usually Okay. Tom is self-conscious in the water. What he himself decides to do is okay, but woe to the person who urges him to try something he considers dangerous. Judy is still young enough to act like water is her natural habitat. She'll coax anyone and everyone to pull her around in the water with a coy smile and "dis a nittoo bitta waddah, peas, Marsa!" (or whoever else is nearby).

Kuling, China
August 29, 1948
2:30 P.M.

Do you smell peanuts? Do you hear cicadas buzzing? Do you hear the workmen singing snatches of rhythmic songs between blows of the hammer and bouts with the saw? Do you feel the sun on your back and see huge red and orange and lavender dahlias at the end of the stone verandah? Hm! So do I.

Our packing isn't nearly finished, but I'm not doing it as I do not do well leaning over duffle-bags these days. We thought our servants would leave this morning, but their boat has been delayed until Monday, so they will not leave until after we do. We are to go down the mountain by chair as usual, boarding our plane at the airport which is between here and Kiukiang. The plane should leave at eleven-thirty, getting us to Nanking by one. Tom is beside himself at this chance to fly, and counting the hours until then.

I'll be very glad when this interminable baby-waiting is over. For some reason I have been much more uncomfortable this time, so sending you a cable telling you of its safe arrival will be a great relief. You asked what I needed. Actually nothing.

Tom and Judy are the ones who need things. The stuff I brought out has stretched as far as it will. Expensive things aren't necessary, but I do yearn over the chance to stand beside a dime-store counter and find balloons, cars, tiny dolls, doll furniture, and that kind of stuff. None of that is available here.

Judy apes as much of Tom as she can manage, and is absolutely in heaven when he lets her know he likes it. She talks very plainly in both English and Chinese, and keeps the cook and amah wrapped around her little finger. She mimics me, going to the kitchen to give the cook orders in Chinese with a perfectly straight face, but with dancing eyes, then chuckles to herself and dances out again.

One of Tom's new passions stops her. He collects all manner of beetles, cicadas, bugs, even crabs. She tries to pretend she does it, too, but cannot quite bear to touch them at the last moment.

The way the currency has been jumping we have almost had to invest it in order to keep its value. The new currency has yet to prove itself. Already a black market has started, though, so we don't have much faith in it. The chief advantage has been that the bills are of a larger denomination, so we don't need a satchel to carry them. Some are twenty, thirty and fifty million each.

Chinese porcelains and camphor chests are less expensive and found in greater variety this year, so we have bought quite a few things for ourselves and for gifts. We bought:

A pair of yellow porcelain plates with nine dragons on them

A set of yellow serving dishes

A pair of green jade figurines

Two pitchers in the shape of Chinese characters

A couple of camphor chests (camphor wood grows up here)

Yesterday we purchased two wool rugs, one eight by ten, the other smaller for the children's room and the study. They are handmade in Changsha, not particularly pretty, but serviceable and unbelievably cheap. Rugs make a lot of difference in the winter in a house where there is no heat.

In the back of our minds always runs the question: will we still be here through the winter? From all the rumblings we hear, that does not seem likely, but we have to go on as though we think we will. First we have to travel off this mountain and back to the Yangtze Valley.

Nanking again
September 1, 1943
(written in pencil on a calendar sheet)

Excuse this paper, but this is all I have out here in the yard and it's too hot to go inside after anything. We started down the mountain at eight a.m. Ben walked ahead of us dressed in T-shirt and shorts, a pack on his back. The children and I followed in two chairs. By ten we were down at the unloading station where we caught the truck with our luggage in it, and all rode together to the airport.

We took off at eleven a.m. after the Navy doctor had insisted on taking pictures of the passengers of the "Stork Express" as they called it. Three of us were pregnant, two weren't, and there were seven children and three husbands, besides the doctor and the crew. The others were all embassy people, good friends of ours. We had a beautiful day to fly—had an almost unobstructed view of the flooded Yangtze River. In some places water was all you could see. It is a serious flood.

We had little breakfast, but ate a packed lunch on the plane. Exactly at 12:30 we settled smoothly down over thatched roofs and rice paddies onto the airstrip outside Nanking. The children and I rode home in an Air Force colonel's car, while Ben came a bit later on the baggage truck.

Though our renters were in Peking, their nineteen-year old son and his five-foot Great Dane were here. Boy, dog, baggage, and servants left yesterday afternoon.

Our amah and the cook arrived this morning by boat. I think they've been having a summer romance, so it is a good thing we are back here where the cook's wife can keep her eye on him.

This Nanking heat is not meant for humans. I am completely miserable. Not four hours after we arrived home, Judy was already blossoming out with prickly heat. The first night none of us could sleep, in spite of using two electric fans. By Tuesday Ben had made a primitive swimming pool under the bamboos in our side yard to keep the children a little cooler. He secured a huge tarp to bamboo poles on braces about two feet above the ground. The water stays in it remarkably well.

Right now I'm sitting on a chair beside them as they "swim" in it. I should have gone to the hospital for a checkup this afternoon, but couldn't face the prospect of the horribly hot, bumpy rickshaw ride. I'll go tomorrow morning if it is any cooler. Our refrigerator and electric fans are certainly appreciated now.

At that point I was interrupted by guests. Since then much has happened.

Wednesday morning I was very sick with diarrhea and vomiting. By nine o'clock labor pains had started, so at noon the rickety Ku Lou ambulance came for me. I climbed in the back of it, clutching one of our electric fans. They dumped me out at the emergency entrance after bumping across the city. Pains continued for twelve hours, then stopped. The doctors poured sulfa into me all day and night, then decided to send me home Thursday afternoon. The fan and my bulky self were packed into a rickshaw, and off we went. Much ado about nothing.

After all that it was disappointing to return with no baby, but the doctors seem to think this little go around should speed things up for me when I go back in a week or so. At least their hospital procedure and many of the personnel are familiar to me now. Besides, nothing was ready here. It has been too hot to bother. Now I'll have time to get the baby's room, clothes, and such all set.

Let's hope your next word from us is a happy cable!

65 Moh Tsou Road
Nanking, Kiangsu
September 16, 1948

No doubt I should be resting now, but I cannot rest until I have put down on paper the hardest thing I've ever had to write. Our darling little Ben, Jr. died last night at eleven o'clock. He was the prettiest baby of all, with dark hair and dark blue eyes, and the same chubby little face Tom and Judy had as babies. He weighed nine pounds.

He was born at 2:45 a.m. on Sunday, September twelfth. Ben had driven me to the hospital in the Methodist car at midnight, and was with me from then on. There was a hassle getting me admitted at that hour, but they finally decided I could stay (!) and escorted me to the maternity section.

The doctor let Ben stand at the head of the operating table holding my hands through the entire delivery. They do not give an anesthetic here, so I was fully conscious the whole time. We shared the first sight of little Ben, and heard his first cry together. He was a beautiful little fellow, and at first we knew only the great joy at his safe arrival and apparent health.

As there was no room immediately available for me, I was left on a cot in the delivery room for the remainder of the night. Meanwhile, four Chinese women had their babies in there. Not much rest was possible, so I was relieved the next morning to be transferred to a room. Usually foreigners are put into a separate section, but the hospital was overcrowded, so I was put in a double room with a young Chinese woman.

No one had time to change linen, so my first day was spent in very soiled sheets.

My roommate didn't want the window open though the heat was stifling. She drank tea, dumping the grounds on the floor from time to time. When they brought her baby in she poured tea into its mouth from the teapot's spout.

When they first brought little Ben to me, I was aware that his color had changed some, but didn't think too much about it. On Monday morning I saw him again, and it was worse. By afternoon he was markedly yellow, so I spoke to Dr. Liu, reminding him that was symptomatic of Rh babies. He answered that he felt it was due to the lack of a vitamin K shot since I had come into the hospital too late to get one!

When he left, I called for Dr. Daniels and Dr. Moffatt. I realized that Dr. Liu had no idea of the seriousness of this symptom, since Chinese have no experience with Rh. What was needed was a complete change of the baby's blood. They started immediately to find the proper kind of blood and someone with knowledge of what to do. Because I knew I had the condition I had read more about it than anyone around me. No time to panic.

It was not until a full day later, at four o'clock on Tuesday afternoon, that Dr. Moffatt was able to locate the necessary type of blood (Rh—type O) which was given by a Sergeant in the American Army Group.

As none of the Ku Lou (Drum Tower) doctors had any knowledge of Rh problems at all, Dr. Moffatt checked with all of the American Army and Navy doctors. He found only one, Dr. Mac Phail from Canada, the Army pediatrician, who had had even the slightest previous experience with it.

On Tuesday night MacPhail and Moffatt attempted the first transfusion on little Ben. Afterwards Dr. Moffatt came up to my room much encouraged by the baby's response. (I had been moved upstairs to a private room on Tuesday morning.) At first they had thought the antibodies might be transmitted through breast feeding, but at this point Dr. MacPhail gave his okay for me to begin nursing.

That night and the next morning the baby was brought to me every four hours. The morning's report showed an encouraging improvement in the red cell count. By noon he started running a temperature. When he was brought for his one o'clock feeding he seemed to be having great difficulty breathing, and his little arms were stiff.

Later on Dr. Daniels stopped in to say that the blood count, in spite of the second transfusion (which had been given at noon) was going down again. I sent for Ben then, for I knew things were getting desperately serious. He came at seven without having had any supper, and unprepared, really, for what had been going on, since he had heard nothing since the encouraging news that morning.

Dr. Moffatt came in at eight o'clock to say that as soon as Dr. MacPhail came they would try again. MacPhail thought the breathing difficulty might be due to the fact that one lung was partially collapsed.

Ben sat with me all evening. Both of us were exhausted. Delle Moffatt came in for a while and took Ben home to give him something to eat. He was back by ten-thirty. A little after eleven a nurse came in with a note from Dr. Moffatt, asking Ben to step down to the office.

In a moment he was back. As he came over to the bed he said, "Well, Peg, we've lost our little boy." In a moment then we asked Dr. Moffatt to come in to tell us what had happened. He came, but he couldn't talk because he was crying. I pulled his head down and kissed him and told him how (continued, 2:00 p.m. Friday, September 17) very grateful we were to him for trying so hard to save the little fellow. He had literally been with the baby almost constantly from Tuesday noon on.

He said that though they had difficulty finding the tiny vein, they had finally been able to give the full injection and thought they had been successful, but suddenly his little heart stopped. Then they tried oxygen and artificial stimulants, but unsuccessfully. The little body had to take too much.

I wanted to go home right then. Facing the nurses and being helpless there seemed too rough to face. But of course that was impossible, so, after I had been given a sedative and was settled for the night, and we had prayed together, Ben left. He told me later that he laid down with Tommy for a long time and then got up and picked Judy out of her crib to hold her close before he went to bed. Those two are triply precious now. Our eyes have been opened to how fortunate we have been in the past.

Thursday morning the doctors readily consented to my request that I be sent home at once. Mary Lu Allen (Stork Express) came to visit me and remained to help get me ready and take me home in their Jeep. Friends have taken Tom and Judy for most meals, and have helped in innumerable ways.

We had a carpenter make a simple little casket. Two friends lined and covered it with two shades of pale blue soft seersucker you had sent me.

At one-fifteen today we had a simple, informal service in our house. Some of the ladies came this morning to decorate the room with flowers sent by friends, the Mission, the Rotary Club, schools, and others. Mr. Rindon played hymns on his record player out in the pantry while people were assembling. Then Ben carried me down the back stairs. Tom and Ben and I sat inside the dining room, just out of sight of the guests in the living room. Ted Romig, Gardner Winn, Tracey Jones, and Pastor Pao all took part in prayers, scripture and poetry reading. It is a Chinese custom to brightly rouge children's lips and cheeks on special occasions. Apparently this was one, for the undertaker had so decorated little Ben. I took my handkerchief and gently wiped it off. Then the little casket was carried out past us, and we came on upstairs.

At this moment the burial service is taking place in the foreign cemetery. Mom, how can anyone stand this? How can I? Tom came upstairs with me, and his penetrating questions have been a great help, really, in keeping my head up.

This has all been very hard, but people have been thoughtful and kind, and a shared burden is lighter. The most difficult part to be reconciled to is the fact that if we had been in America this need not have happened. Rh difficulties are almost unknown among Chinese for some reason. When the emergency came there was no one who knew exactly what to do. You will remember that my Dr. in Berkeley gave me biweekly blood tests before Judy arrived. He was preparing for this very thing. Had that been done this time and the baby taken when the first antibodies began to appear in my blood, or even had they checked his blood at birth and transfused correctly within a few minutes or hours, he'd have been saved.

That is bitter to know, but may as well be faced. There are no facilities here for determining the presence of the antibodies, so no one acted until the condition had advanced far enough to be seen in physical symptoms. And that was too far. If we are ever to have another child it must only be in America!

Your cable was delivered to us as we sat at breakfast this morning. It helped immensely towards getting through this day to know that you, too, were aware of and sharing our sorrow, though you are so far away. The words of comfort in the service were very real, and made us so very deeply thankful that we know this source of strength for times like this.

I am feeling fairly strong, though of course the strain of these past days cannot help but take their toll. I'll rest for a while and soon be all right again. Tom and Judy are both well. Judy has spent this day away from home, but will be back tonight for supper. Tom we allowed to go to the service for many reasons, among them the fact that he has picked up a lot of queer notions about funerals and death from his too-alert observation of Chinese customs. He wondered which of us would put white rags on our heads and who would be blowing the horns, for example. I hope he has a quite different conception now.

Thank you for letting me use you as a support during this dark hour and a half. I still cannot face the empty nursery, but will try tomorrow.

Nanking, China
September 27, 1948

Judy and Tom are gradually signing off for the night. Ben is downstairs in conversation with, Chang Ping Wen, the assistant at Han Chung Church, and I am dressed for bed, listening to the *Nutcracker Suite* via borrowed record and player beside my bed.

Your letters arrived. We thank you so much for them. It has been such a strength to feel the love and prayers of not only our own family, but the many, many friends who have generously written notes of sympathy. I never realized what these notes and the extra warm pressure of hand clasps and even the flowers meant. We have been all but overwhelmed by the evidence of real affection from many unexpected sources.

The note we appreciated the most came from one of our senior missionaries who has been difficult to work with in many ways, but who showed a depth of sympathy and understanding that moved us deeply. He and his wife lost a little three-year-old boy, their only son, twenty years ago—in Nanking.

I have been much slower about getting around this time than I had planned, but apparently shock takes its toll. Although I was able to attend the funeral, I felt the effects most of that week, and still haven't much pep. Fortunately I don't have to worry about caring physically for children, house, or meals as I would if this weren't China, so I've been staying down much of the time, going downstairs for meals only and occupying myself with sewing and other slow jobs that can be done in our room.

The past three days I've felt much better. I even rickshawed to call on Nary Lu Allen at the Army Hospital where her baby girl was born. Another friend had a boy the same day. They are in the same room, and are the ones who shared the ride on the "Stork Special" plane from Kuling. After seeing them, I went on to church at the university, then had four guests for supper, so it was quite a day. I did get very tired, but feel fine today.

Our amah has been wonderful. She not only keeps the children happy, but is very clever with her needle. With her expert help my wardrobe is acquiring a hint or two of the "New Look" via let-down hems.

We miss little Ben now more now than ever. At first the shock stunned us. Later when nerves and numbed heart begin to tackle life "as it was" again, the desolate emptiness is a mockery. The knowledge that our baby died unnecessarily is inexpressibly bitter to accept. Never again will we be foolish enough to risk such priceless stakes in China.

Incidentally, we're told we are scheduled for furlough in 1950, possibly even 1949. That is assuming conditions here improve enough for us to be able to stay until then. Right now that is looking doubtful.

Nanking, China
October 6, 1948

The house is very quiet, but the noises from the street haven't diminished from their daytime intensity even though it is after eight p.m. Judy and Tom have been asleep for about fifteen minutes, so I've been trying to catch up on correspondence.

Ben left at five-thirty with a group of five Chinese delegates for a conference of youth workers starting tomorrow morning in Soochow, and extending through until next Wednesday. He had arranged for me to go to Soochow on the train for the last two days of the conference and then on to Shanghai and, we hope, Hangchow, before coming home again. So there is something to anticipate.

This week has been filled with meetings. I went to the International Women's Club at the Dutch Embassy on Monday afternoon. That night we invited the session board of Han Chung Church to meet here for a powwow over the new Youth Centers. They came. All sixteen of them. They stayed until eleven p.m.

Yesterday a friend in the AAG and his wife asked us to dinner at their lovely home. She gave me a bottle of shampoo and a package of cottage cheese. The latter the first we've had in China. The former, something I needed desperately. The week little Ben died, this same lady came over and brought me a pretty package containing a lovely nightie, a Fischer slip, some sachet, and two pair of nylons.

Today I merely loafed, except for helping a little at a Bible class this afternoon. Tomorrow I have been asked to "pour" at a tea the mission is having to greet newcomers and say farewell to Dr. and Mrs. Moffatt who are scheduled to sail October 20 for Korea.

Saturday morning is a meeting of the YWCA Board, followed by a luncheon. Saturday afternoon the Ginling faculty are having a tea to welcome new music faculty members. I've been asked to "pour" there, too. People are still going out of their way to be kind.

This sounds like, and is, a busy week, but it seems slow and pleasantly leisurely compared with the pace I kept last spring. I'm feeling fine again, but still resting a lot, as I tire easily.

Tom has started Kindergarten at the Army Advisory Group school on Monday and loves it. All Army buses (he rides one to and from school) have one or more Sikh guards. These men look quite fierce in their turbans and beards, but the children love them. I asked Tom whether these guards speak English. He said: "Of course they do. When we get on the bus they always say, "Hello! Sit DOWN.." He now pretends he is a Sikkh, and is convinced it is only a matter of time before his "beards come dripping out." Tonight he said, with the air of one making a not-to-be-disputed statement: "A woman is an old girl."!

LIFE AND DEATH IN NANKING

Nanking, China
October 19, 1948

A week ago Sunday night I took the night train for Soochow. Sleeper. Elegant. Just like a Pullman in the States. I had my own berth and everything. It certainly was different from the wild, dirty, crowded coach ride when we arrived in 1946. What a world of experiences China has shown us since then. Knowing the language and knowing Chinese people now changes how everything looks.

Ben met me at the Soochow station in the cold, gray dawn. It was five-twenty in the morning. We hired a rickshaw for me, while he rode a borrowed bicycle back the two miles through countryside to the school compound where the conference of youth workers was being held. As no one was up at that hour, we sat and talked quietly until they were.

That day I went on an all day boat ride on the Soochow Canal with a group of local people. Soochow is like Venice in that canals take the place of streets. The buildings are ancient, mostly gray, but graceful and surrounded with gardens and trees. There are hundreds of boats of all sizes and shapes on the canal. Many people spend their whole lives on these boats. They never set foot on land. That is also true of the moat which nearly surrounds the city of Nanking.

On Thursday at four in the morning we left the conference to catch the five-twenty train to Shanghai. We made it, after a cold hike and ride (I had a rickshaw) through early morning fog. The train got us to Shanghai at seven a.m.

We spent the day shopping and calling on friends, lunched at the Sino-British Club, went to a movie, and then took a taxi to the Sidney Anderson's for the night. Shanghai is so different from Nanking. It is crowded with people from most countries of the world in addition to its Chinese population. There are areas set apart for foreigners where buildings seem to belong in Europe, rather than China. Then there are steaming, smelly alleys where the American expression "teeming multitudes" seems most apt.

Shops of every description, where clothing, art, food, trinkets, coffins, paper products, herbs, medicines, and many many more wares are jammed and piled on top of one another. Along the waterfront, called the "Bund" ships from dozens of countries are berthed. Bustling around them, like fish darting here and there are sampans, junks, and smaller craft whose owners (?) ceaselessly work at selling their contents to those on board the larger craft. The smell of rotting fish and whatever else is overwhelming.

On Friday morning after an early breakfast we took a train for Hangchow. We arrived there at noon, and were met by a friend who escorted us to his home for lunch. After lunch we set out for Ling Yin, a Buddhist temple on a mountainside. We took our time and ambled around. Hangchow is gorgeous. Scholars and artists have come there for centuries.

There is a long, long lake bordered by magnificent homes and gardens. Since it is fall the brilliant foliage was a perfect foil for the scarlet pillars of some of the homes and pagodas. We have so few trees of any kind in Nanking that the abundance of them in Hangchow was a delight to see.

As we wandered about we happened to be in one temple while a crowded service honoring the departed mother of a young man was taking place. Fascinating. The temple itself was beautiful. There were gilded figures of various friendly and unfriendly deities nearly eighty feet tall in several of the larger rooms. These figures are scary-looking, but as art are most impressive.

Saturday we shopped a little, and then set out for another temple, this one Taoist. This involved climbing, too. It was situated on a mountain top (actually a hill), which we took slowly, enjoying the panoramic view as we climbed it. We ate lunch up there, and then hiked down the other side to the lake, where we took a gondola to the several islands, and thence back to the city once more.

We stopped to see an ancient mission house. After all the beautiful buildings we had been viewing this was truly a monstrosity. How can the Chinese put up with us? After an early supper we were off to catch the seven p.m. train for Shanghai which got there at eleven-ten. We grabbed our bags and ran for the Nanking train, due to leave at eleven-ten. We made it, but had to sit up all night, as the berths were all filled.

Back in Nanking at seven a.m. we came directly home to find cook giving Judy her breakfast in solitary grandeur. She was elated to see us. Ben went right to the Joneses' for Tom, and got another warm reception. At eleven we went to Han Chung to Church, taking Judy. Right after lunch we went to sleep, getting up in time for church at the university. Then home, supper, and to bed. Yesterday I spent cleaning our third floor for a guest from the New York office who is due to arrive tonight for a three-week stay with us! Onward and upward!

Another crisis is ahead in Chinese politics. We are all holding our breath. The new currency has already flopped, and merchants are hiding their merchandise rather than obey price rulings. Flour, rice, sugar, and other staples are impossible to find in the city.

The box with Judy's doll came the day I left for Soochow. Cook is going down this afternoon to get it from the Post Office. You needn't worry now about things not getting through to us. Nothing seems to be lost in transit anymore. The Post Office Department is the best in the whole Nationalist Government. Duty is high, but in cases of things not obtainable here, is worth it. Nylon and rayon goods are now not allowed in.

Ku Lou Hospital AGAIN
October 30, 1948

This is being written from my bed in Ku Lou Hospital to which I was brought by ambulance last Monday for an emergency appendectomy. I had been singing a solo at a university meeting when sharp pains hit me. I went home to bed, but the pains kept getting worse. Ben had a fever of 105° (malaria attack) at the time, so didn't know much about what was happening to me. I sent word with the coolie for an ambulance.

As my blood count wasn't right, they delayed operating until Tuesday afternoon at five. A Chinese surgeon, oldish, very kind, officiated. I was given a spinal anesthetic, so was conscious throughout. Dr. Daniels held my head and talked to me during the operation. I could watch them in an overhead reflector.

The first night was pure agony. They were feeding me intravenously. During the night, while I was alone, an old Chinese janitor came into my room. He was curious and poked all the equipment, jarring the needle out of place, shooting the liquid into the tissues rather than into my vein.

My arm quickly started to swell painfully. I summoned a nurse, and asked her to get the doctor. She said he could not be disturbed until morning. After a couple of hours my arm had gotten nearly twice normal size and hurt like crazy. I called the nurse again and threw a fit, telling her I was about to die and it would be her fault if she did not get the doctor immediately.

An hour later he came, and was shocked at what had happened. He fixed it up and ordered morphine for the pain. Again I had trouble convincing anyone that I knew anything. Morphine does me no good. About Wednesday noon they finally believed me, ordered codeine instead, so at last I began to rest a little.

Now it is Saturday at six in the morning. I'm much better now, though slow to move and terribly weak. The nurses have been great. There is one older lady, a Miss Kung, who took care of me when I was here in September. She putters around, treats me like a little child, and does everything she can to make me comfortable.

Ben has nearly recovered from malaria. Quinine works fast, but leaves you weak and useless. He brought the children to see me yesterday. That was the first I'd seen of any of them for five days. Tom was avidly curious about the "hole they chopped" in my tummy.

We are more and more worried about conditions here. Outstation people are pouring into Nanking. If any of us stays through the winter, it will be under extremely crowded conditions.

Apparently the fact that a Communist takeover is imminent has affected the Nanking food supply. Meal after meal here in the hospital, we are served nothing but liver (for meat). Maybe the rest of the animals go to feed troops. Who knows? Merchants are hanging onto their rice as the prices skyrocket. People are hungry. They mob the stores. That is a rice riot. It is scary. The riots are beginning to be more frequent and more serious. We worry about their possible outcome, but no one is quite sure what is happening.

Meanwhile, the package you sent is still in the Post Office. We've been too broke to retrieve it. Our check came this week, so now we can get it.

PEGGY KORDICK

Nanking, China
Ku Lou Hospital
November 5, 1948

Do you mind my weeping on your shoulder? This morning I am away down at the bottom of a barrel of discouragement. First, last night I went by proxy through the grueling process of childbearing. In the room next to mine is a good friend, Mary Kay Ding, wife of a university professor. She had a baby last night, and I went through the whole experience with her. I'm tired and nervously wrought up, and, as I said, blue—as—Tahoe!

People are beginning to call us Mr. and Mrs. Job. And right now "O Lord, How Long?" is beating through my brain. Today they remove the sutures from my appendectomy. I was to have gone home tomorrow, but yesterday Dr. Daniels discovered that I have Amoebic Dysentery, so I may have to stay a while. This when Ben looks like a scarecrow after his recent malaria bout, Judy has a severe case of round worms and hasn't eaten for four days, and Tom has bronchitis. It's just too much. I simply am tired of it all.

The national picture doesn't cheer anyone up either. People are to be evacuated at once from Peking. That means our house will soon be bulging at the seams with extra people, and our cook has not been able the past three weeks to buy enough food for our own household. There has been no meat, no flour, no sugar, no eggs, and no rice to be had. Now some of those things are slowly becoming available, but at unbelievable prices. Butter is $16 GY or $4 US! No one seems to know whether we'll have to leave when the present government folds, but its fall is imminent now—expected daily.

Before I came to the hospital I found out that the government has "requested" all women to donate any gold jewelry they may have to the treasury in an effort to stabilize the currency. Many of my friends in the YWCA, schools, and elsewhere gave even their wedding bands. I wonder where it will really go. Most of us think the government is simply stealing it.

Probably our greatest danger lies from possible rioting and disorder following the Kuomintang collapse. The presence of the American Army in such numbers is our greatest safeguard. There are so many questions to be faced. If we have to leave Nanking—where then? West China? Or home?

I'm so tired and exhausted physically and nervously that the prospect of rushing from place to place seems more than I could take at this point. We would probably choose home if we had a choice. Ben describes his own state as battle fatigue, and that is probably what it is for us both.

Well, gloom, gloom, gloom! I'm sure to regret writing this, but as of now...

Next morning, November 4th six a.m.

Things don't look quite so dark this morning. The sutures were removed successfully yesterday. As Dr. Daniels is in no hurry to start the dysentery treatment I'll go home today. That in itself is cheering. Hsing Hsin brought Judy in to see me yesterday afternoon. Although Judy looked like any animated, pink-cheeked doll, she nearly broke my heart. During my weeks of disability she has turned completely to Hsing Hsin and treats me like a stranger.

No, Judy doesn't yet have her doll. That package has been in the Post Office nearly a month. The Post Office is miles across town. Once we sent the cook for it, but failed to send enough money to cover the duty charge.

Tom is counting the days until his birthday. Time is so short I may not have time to have a cowboy suit made for him as I had planned to do. The red shirt you sent will be perfect to top it off. The Chinese line their winter garments with sheepskin: I plan to attach some of that to denim pants for "chaps." We have an old felt hat I'll make into a sombrero. Presto!

Just now my Miss Kung came in. Yesterday the hospital gave all its female staff winter coats from bales of clothing sent from America. They used an awfully dumb system. They numbered the coats, then had the women draw numbers. Regardless of fit, the coat was given to whatever person held its number. Miss Kung got one that is far too small. Though she is small, she can't even get into it.

There is one at home that I've been saving for someone special. I told her I'd send it to her. She's pathetically pleased, and cannot do enough to express her appreciation. I hope this won't be another disappointment for her. It is a black wool coat and too large for me, so should fit her.

Now they're coming to give me a bath. It is seven a.m. and I've finished eating, so I must finish this quickly. This looks like a beautiful day—and I feel fine, so don't be too upset by the other part of this letter. Tom is back in school again, and Judy is almost okay.

The last I heard yesterday, Truman was ahead. Wonder which way it turned out.

Nanking, China
Sunday, November 7, 1943

The other part of this letter was written long enough ago to be stale now, and since it was not mailed and you may be upset over the recent news you have been hearing, I must get something off to you today.

I came home from the hospital Thursday afternoon. Needless to say, I was plenty happy to! I don't feel at all well. My side hurts awfully sometimes, and I have picked up a bad cold from Judy or a weather change or something. I have stayed fairly quiet, but with three house guests, everything in a dither, and the servants all rattled over the situation in China, neither of us can follow the routine which would be best from a health point of view.

Things have gone from bad to much worse so quickly that most people haven't caught up yet. The embassy has issued its first warning to Americans who "have no compelling reason to stay" to leave while trains are still running between here and the coast. Hence, most of the Army dependents are packing and hastily getting out.

The American school has closed, as the teachers are being sent home. Tommy is heartbroken. "All right," he announced at breakfast, "if they hab any kindergartens in America I'll just go dere."

It is difficult to tell you accurately what the situation is. It changes by the minute. Please know that so far we are in no danger at all. It is true that the Communist armies are headed now for Nanking and it is only a matter of time before they get here. The thing we as missionaries do not know is whether we will be permitted to stay on through the change in government which now seems inevitable.

Foreigners in Tsinan, which recently fell for the second time, seem to have been well treated. Communist leaders have been broadcasting to the effect that foreigners don't necessarily have to leave. What this means we aren't quite sure. We are here, not primarily as Americans, but as Christians, and we must do whatever seems best from a Christian viewpoint.

Naturally the Army people must leave. Their dependents have no real business here, and because the Army men have been acting as advisors to the Kuomintang against the Communists, they will no longer be welcome. (Understatement!)

Not many of the embassy families are leaving yet. Still, all of us must be prepared to leave in a hurry when it seems necessary. I have gone through trunks, discarding rafts of stuff by giving it away. I would rather give it to those who can use it than to have it wantonly destroyed later—as has happened elsewhere. We sent notes to several schools to have students come take their pick of clothes, books, paper, and whatever. They have been streaming in and out of here for several days.

We are packing our most valuable portable things plus items we had purchased for gifts and are sending them to you with one of the Army families. That way we won't lose absolutely everything in case we do have to drop everything and run, later. We'll ask you to keep them for us.

Ben teases me about "spreading propaganda" regarding our own possible return to America. I do not deny that events this fall have left me with very little appetite for further troubles. However, I do not want to do anything which might harm the job we came here to do. Obviously we will not risk the children's welfare.

You will have to sit tight, pray hard, and know that we will be following not only our own best judgment, but the leading of the Heavenly Father in whatever decisions we make in the days ahead. You had better advise people not to send us Christmas boxes. Later, maybe.

Shanghai, China
November 19, 1948

If you note the dateline, you will know that at least some of what you've been hearing lately is true! Days have flown by in such a haze that I really have trouble remembering what day of the week it is — much more what date.

Last week one day we were suddenly given notice that we were to leave on an American LST for Shanghai, sans belongings. Then we were told first one thing and then another in a succession of word-of-mouth messages that left us spinning. Since we have no telephone, messengers came many times with "chit books." The final upshot was that we boarded an American destroyer escort on the Yangtze on Sunday evening about five after days of feverish packing—and wrenching farewells from Chinese friends and servants.

We had worked around the clock, deciding which were irreplaceable items, mostly Chinese dishes, bundled them as best we could in towels and washcloths, and packed them in Chinese carved camphor chests and a few footlockers, not sure from hour to hour whether we'd get to take them.

When the orders to evacuate suddenly came, we were told we could take anything ready to go. Coolies slammed the stuff end-over-end down our front steps, loaded them on a truck out front, and we were off.

After a bumpy ride to the Yangtze River, we boarded a United States destroyer escort which had been sent in from Shanghai to "rescue" us. Accommodations for men and women were separate, so Ben took Tom to bunk with him, while Judy and I were assigned a third and second-tier bunk respectively.

All was understandable bedlam, reporters shooting pictures, children screaming, people milling about. We were too weary and numb to be concerned about Communist gun batteries reputedly across the river. My appendectomy incision hasn't healed, and I ripped it open lifting chunky Judy into her bunk.

About 250 Americans were taken to Shanghai on this ship. We got here Monday about five p.m., then were directed to Mary Farnam School for girls. It is the same place we stayed when I first arrived in

1946. Here we are again, freezing in two rooms in a girls' dorm. (We only eat at the mission house.)

Naturally, we are in a daze, not to say a stupor over the rapidity of the successive blows we've been dealt lately. This evacuation has a dreamlike quality about it anyway. Life goes on as usual on the surface, with only acute food shortages and curfews keeping people off the streets to indicate anything is wrong.

The last days we were in Nanking were tense and unreal. Riots had been bad, but with the clamping down of martial law, had stopped. Swarms of Nationalist planes were overhead carrying government officials and their families and treasures to Taiwan.

There will be much to tell you. When we sail is still uncertain, but it should be within the next two weeks. In the meantime we are comfortable, but not in even remote danger. We're too bewildered to plan for more than a day at a time, but suppose we'll head for your place if we ever get out of this mesa. After that....? Who knows?

Dr. Moffatt is here in Shanghai, waiting to go to Korea, so he came and looked at the gory mess my infected, ripped open incision has become. He decided he had to stitch it up, and proceeded to do just that, sans anesthetic, here in this freezing dormitory room. WHEW! I'm grateful to have it taken care of, but not for the experience. It should start healing now.

Now if we can just be assigned to a ship—any ship!

Post Script: November 20, 1948

This morning I've tried again unsuccessfully to get us on the General Buckner, sailing Monday, but now have decided it is impossible. The mission assures that we are definitely on the next ship, which we hear will sail the 27th or before. These transports do not take freight, so we'll have to make other arrangements about the trunks we were able to bring from Nanking. We also have to have shots.

Lots of other people are being sent elsewhere in China, to the Philippines, and to Japan, but we are to go home our health problems were the deciding factor.

Except for necessary errands, we stay right in the girls' school compound. There are almost no students here right now, and only a skeleton faculty. We "refugees" have the place almost to ourselves. There is time to think, but somehow I cannot. My brain and senses are numb. The Chinese people we see are closed and withdrawn. Some may imagine they know what is ahead, but my guess is that few actually do.

I cannot allow myself to speculate on how little our presence here has mattered. What was it all about?

That was the last letter, scribbled hastily on a torn calendar page. Things had been too madly scrambled the last few hours for even the Great Communicator to handle writing any more.

They sailed from Shanghai on a converted U.S. Army hospital ship, the *Republic*. Hsing Hsin, the amah, and Liu Shih Fu, the Cook, had somehow made their way to Shanghai and begged to be taken along. That was impossible of course. One more heartache seeing them waving, with tears flowing, as the *Republic* pulled away. What would happen to those dear, loyal people? Our friends? The students? What dark road was ahead for them? The shadows of tumultuous change loomed over everyone.

As the ship moved towards the ocean, darkness soon hid the city from view. Peggy was standing on the stern straining for a last look. Suddenly, the water in the *Republic's* wake was coated with the ship's garbage. She had been so long immersed in China's studious thrift that her reaction was total shock.

It was said that five thousand Americans were aboard. Could they ever take part in the life of China again? She remembered Dr. Mills and his stories of countless previous upheavals. What was the magnet which always drew people back?

It was China!